CATHEDRAL ON CALIFORNIA STREET

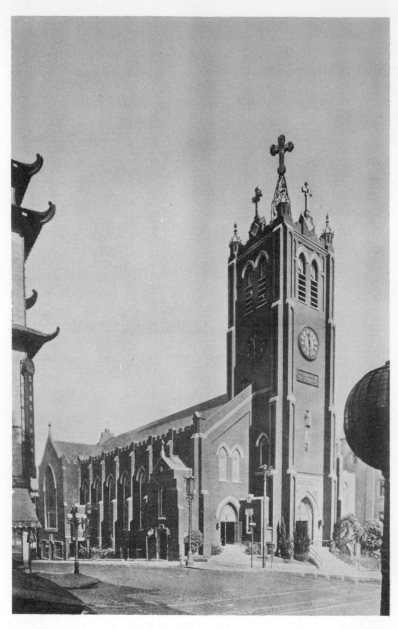

Old St. Mary's Church
San Francisco
1951

Cathedral
on
California Street

The Story of
St. Mary's Cathedral, San Francisco
1854-1891
And of Old St. Mary's, a Paulist Church
1894-1951

By
THOMAS DENIS McSWEENEY

ACADEMY OF CALIFORNIA CHURCH HISTORY
FRESNO, CALIFORNIA
1952

Nihil Obstat:
AMANCIO RODRIGUEZ
CENSOR LIBRORUM

Imprimatur:
† A. J. WILLINGER
COADJUTOR BISHOP OF MONTEREY-FRESNO
February 1, 1952

Academy of California Church History
PUBLICATION NUMBER FOUR

COPYRIGHT BY
ACADEMY OF CALIFORNIA CHURCH HISTORY
1952

LITHOGRAPHED IN THE U.S.A.

FOREWORD

It is a privilege to introduce this story of San Francisco's Cathedral on California Street to all those interested in the rich and full heritage bequeathed us by the Faith of our Fathers here by the western sea. Too long have we been unmindful of the story of men and women, of places and events, which have marked the progress of Catholicism in the West during the more than a century which has now elapsed since the discovery of gold in 1848. This publication represents the first fruits of the Graduate School of the University of San Francisco, and it is hoped that its publication marks but the beginning of such scholarly offerings. The History Department of the University has instituted a long range program looking to just such an accomplishment and it is felt that the program should win both acceptance and favor from those concerned with the preservation of the saga of Catholicism in its Californian and Western phase. In this regard, especial interest is hoped for from our various religious communities, for there is no one of them which does not have at least a chapter or two to contribute to the broader history of Catholicism in this region which will one day emerge from just such studies as the present.

The Most Reverend Thomas K. Gorman, D.D., Bishop of Reno, Nevada, recently wrote in the Catholic Historical Review:

A complete history of the Catholic Church in California and in the other states of the Pacific Slope during the decades immediately following the Gold Rush has still to take form. Indeed, it can scarcely be written until a whole series of local studies and biographies has been prepared from source materials all too scarce and none too well preserved. Some of this spade work is being done, but not enough. Here is an almost unexplored field for competent research by Catholic historians.

Bishop Gorman's thoughtful words find support in the lines kindly contributed by another member of the Hierarchy of the West, the Most Reverend Robert J. Armstrong, D.D., Bishop of

V

129374

Sacramento, as a foreword to my *Eloquent Indian: the Life of James Bouchard, California Jesuit.* Bishop Armstrong there wrote:

May I express the hope that this story of an ELOQUENT INDIAN *may inspire others to apply themselves to the rewarding task of re-creating some other portion of the Catholic past of this Frontier of Faith in the Far West.*

This present study, a publication of the Academy of California Church History, is a modest attempt to fulfill the scholarly desires of Their Excellencies of Reno and Sacramento. While it is not claimed that the study represents a definitive account of San Francisco's first Cathedral, for circumstances have made this highest of all goals unattainable at this time, it is believed that, despite imperfections which the critic will not fail to detect, Mr. McSweeney's volume represents a solid and scholarly contribution to the all too scarce literature of the subject.

Finally, I should like to congratulate Mr. McSweeney, for his shall ever be the distinction of being the pioneer in the publications we envision. I should like, too, to express my sincere appreciation to the Right Reverend James Culleton, Chancellor of the Diocese of Monterey-Fresno and President of the Academy of California Church History, for making this publication possible; Monsignor Culleton is already in the debt of California Catholic scholars because of a long sustained interest which has now proven itself by the publications of the Academy which he has founded. May this story of the Cathedral on California Street be succeeded, as time and circumstances permit, by a goodly number of other such monographs which will, eventually, go into the making of an authoritative and enduring account of the Catholic Church in El Dorado and the West.

John Bernard McGloin, S.J.,
History Department,
University of San Francisco.

VI

PREFACE

The lumbering grey bus ground slowly down California Street from Nob Hill and swung left to go up Grant Avenue. To the San Franciscan who stood on the curb and waited for the sight-seeing bus to make the turn it was a familiar sight, as familiar as the cable cars that crawled up and down the steep California hills, as familiar as the red brick building on the corner of California Street and Grant Avenue. As the bus passed, crowding its bulk through the narrow street that is the heart of San Francisco's Chinatown, the San Franciscan glanced up at the large clock on the tower of the building beside him and hurried on his way. It was the press of business and not the familiar inscription on the building, "Son, Observe the time and fly from evil," that hastened his steps. In a few brief moments his steps had carried him beyond the building, and Old St. Mary's Church was crowded out of his mind by the problems of the moment. But any study of the San Francisco that was, when gold dust was the coin of commerce, must necessarily involve St. Mary's. This church on the corner of California Street and Grant Avenue was San Francisco's First Cathedral from 1854 until 1891.

The present name of this Church, Old St. Mary's, may seem to be unusual. However, it is not entirely unique or unusual that the passage of time in a diocese should bring about a change in the location of a Cathedral Church. In San Francisco, though, we have the unusual circumstance of having the first Cathedral dedicated to St. Mary, Ever Virgin and Conceived Without Sin, and its successor also dedicated to the Blessed Virgin Mary. For purposes of clarity, we shall here trace the history of the Cathedral that was, the seat of the Bishop in the Diocese and later Archdiocese.

On February 4, 1851, Rt. Rev. Joseph Sadoc Alemany, (1814-1888), reached Monterey and established himself there using San Carlos, the parish church of the Pueblo of Monterey, as his pro-Cathedral. It may be said of these early days that although Bishop Alemany established San Carlos as his pro-Cathedral, the need of episcopal visitation and administration was so great, and the extent of his diocese so large that he officiated more often throughout his diocese than in his pro-Cathedral. The Church of San Carlos remained his pro-Cathedral until he changed his residence on July 9, 1853, to St. Francis of Assisi Church, San Francisco. St. Francis

VII

Church became the new episcopal residence until the dedication of St. Mary's Cathedral on December 25, 1854. St. Mary's was the first Cathedral of the Archdiocese of San Francisco and remained such until 1891. After Archbishop Alemany resigned (1884) and subsequently departed for Spain, the construction of a new Cathedral was commenced by his successor, Archbishop Patrick W. Riordan, (1841-1914), who transferred his residence and officiated at St. John Baptist Church on Eddy Street, from June 24, 1885, until the dedication of St. Mary's Cathedral on Van Ness Avenue at O'Farrell Street on January 11, 1891. This present study will deal with the first Cathedral of San Francisco, St. Mary's, 1854 to 1891.

As one looks at the picture of life in San Francisco during the period from 1850 to 1890, he is struck with the importance which this edifice, St. Mary's, played in San Francisco Catholic life. It would not be an overstatement to say that it was the heart and center of Catholic life in San Francisco for almost half a century. From the first its prominent position is evident. It was described as the most striking building in the new city. Erected on a natural eminence overlooking the bustling community, standing above the cluster of smaller buildings, it was pointed to with pride by both Catholics and non-Catholics alike as evidence of the city's growth and maturity.

In attempting to trace its life and influence upon the city which it overshadowed, I have many times found evidence of valuable contributions which St. Mary's, as an institution in itself, has made to the life of the city of San Francisco. Unfortunately, a portion of the evidence of this contribution has been lost by the destruction of an unknown but considerable part of the records in the holocaust of fire and earthquake that leveled so much of San Francisco on April 18, 1906. Recourse has been made by the author to the files of contemporary daily and weekly newspapers, as well as those of certain other pertinent periodicals of the day. The most important contribution to my story was gained from an intensive and exhaustive study of *The Monitor,* which, since 1858 to the present time, has been the leading Catholic newspaper of the Archdiocese of San Francisco. Recourse was also had to the files of the San Francisco newspapers at the San Francisco Public Library, The Bancroft Library at Berkeley, The California Room of The State Library, Sacramento. *The Catholic Guardian,* a short-lived San Francisco Catholic paper, as well as *The Freeman's Journal* furnished a few valuable items.

In the treatment of St. Mary's Cathedral the material will be presented in four parts. *The first part* will quite logically deal with the beginnings and construction of the Cathedral. *Secondly,* I will show through the organizations which attached themselves to the Cathedral how its influence spread throughout the entire community. Such organizations as schools, literary societies, temperance societies, and cultural societies found their center and strength in the basement meeting place of St. Mary's Cathedral. It is not an over-statement to say that this basement of St. Mary's Cathedral brought to the Catholic and non-Catholic of San Francisco intellectual, cultural, and moral development not surpassed by any other site in San Francisco. Although Platt's Hall was truly the more common meeting place of interested groups of the citizenry, nevertheless, St. Mary's Cathedral was the scene of some of the most important meetings held by the people of San Francisco. *The third part* will be a treatment of some of the great days and events which concerned St. Mary's Cathedral. Such events as the struggle to keep California within the Union, the episcopal consecration in 1881 of Father Patrick Manogue, (1831-1895), as Coadjutor Bishop of Grass Valley, the obsequies of Pope Pius IX, were events which directly concerned the welfare of the State of California and the City of San Francisco in particular. *The fourth* and final material to be developed will be the reasons for, and building of, a new Cathedral and the end of St. Mary's as San Francisco's first Cathedral.

I would like to express my gratitude to Sister Gertrude Mary, S.H.N., Professor of History, College of the Holy Names, Lake Merritt, Oakland, California, for permitting me to use her file of photostat material concerning Archbishop Alemany and the microfilm file of *The Freeman's Journal.* I wish to thank Peter T. Conmy for the use of his unpublished manuscript, "A History of St. Francis Parish." To the staff of *The Monitor,* the staff of the Bancroft Library at Berkeley, and the staff of the California Room of the State Library at Sacramento, I would also like to express my gratitude for their active cooperation in this study.

In an especial manner, I would like to express my gratitude to the director of this study, the Reverend John B. McGloin, S. J., Ph. D., of the University of San Francisco, whose scholarly zeal and patient help has given the encouragement to see this work to its conclusion. To the Reverend Peter M. Dunne, S.J., Ph. D., of the University of San Francisco, who first awoke in me the active interest in the heritage we have received, I wish also to express my appreciation in an especial manner. Finally, I would like to express my gratitude to my wife, Edna. The weeks we spent together in the libraries and archives of Northern California seeking to breathe life again into the story of the first Cathedral of San Francisco have made her as familiar with St. Mary's Cathedral history as myself. It was fitting, therefore, that on July 1, 1950, we were married in the church that we have both come to love and revere, St. Mary's, San Francisco's first Cathedral.

Thomas Denis McSweeney

San Francisco, California
July 1, 1951.

TABLE OF CONTENTS

AMERICAN DAWN
BY THE WESTERN SEA:
The Beginning of the "American" Period
of Roman Catholicism in California
1848-1849

St. Mary's Cathedral
San Francisco
about 1856

Bishop Diego y Moreno, 1785-1846 ...

One of the greatest sources of solace to the laborer in the vineyard of Christ is the hope that from his sweat and toil the growth of later years may spring. But to a few this comfort is denied and in its place is offered only dismal, heart-eroding failure. Such was the condition of the temporal affairs of the church that lay on all sides of the Rt. Rev. Francisco Garcia Diego y Moreno (1), first Bishop of Both Californias, as he lay on his death bed April 30, 1846. His high hopes for his diocese—a seminary, a new cathedral, a vigorous laity—all these had been ground down under the opposition of Mexican officials, the poverty of the majority of the faithful, and the unequal fight of the few padres against distance, dispersion, and numbers of the faithful. Through the machinations of officialdom and of the "paisanos" the cause of religion had been beaten down to the dull monotony of California life as it existed in 1846. (2)

But scarcely had Bishop Diego, sick of heart but yet valiant, returned to offer his account of his stewardship to his God, when the tide began to turn. Breaking through the fastness of the mountains of the Sierras and rolling ashore on the tide of the Pacific came the "Gringo." Perhaps he was not always sympathetic to the missionaries, but he brought vitality, energy, change. He would lay the foundation for the civilization that gold would soon bring swarming upon these alien shores. With the onrush of thousands after the twenty-fourth of January, 1848, a date which changed the course of history for the whole Pacific slope, the dark night of the Catholic Church in California was yielding to the bright promise of the morning under American rule.

Political and Religious Conditions of 1848 ...

Although a brighter dawn of Catholicism in California was coming, gold brought turbulent times out of which order came but slowly. John White Geary (1819-1873), (3) who was elected, August 1, 1849, Alcalde of San Francisco, in summing up conditions in San Francisco as he saw them, addressed an assemblage of citizens as follows:

At this time we are without a dollar in the public treasury, and it is to be feared the city is greatly in debt. You have neither an office for your magistrate nor any other public edifice. You are without the means of confining a prisoner for an hour. Neither have you a place to shelter

3

while living, sick and unfortunate strangers who may be cast upon our shores, or to bury them when dead. Public improvements are unknown in San Francisco, for the protection of property, or for the maintenance of order (4).

These words were addressed to the citizens of the future city of San Francisco in August, 1849. The condition of the Catholic Church in San Francisco was in an equally disorganized state. In a memorandum written by Lieutenant James A. Hardie (1823-1876), (5) while on tour of duty in California with the Third Artillery, U. S. Army, the situation in San Francisco is described as follows:

From the conversation I had with you, a few days since upon the condition of the Catholic Church in California and particularly of the wants of the Catholic population in San Francisco, I am induced to be-lieve that the interest you manifested upon the occasion would lead you upon your arrival in the U. S., to make such representation in valuable quarters, and to use such endeavors as would make known the real con-dition of Catholic matters here and would tend to apply a remedy to what you believed to be existing evils.

I am too well acquainted with the position and growing importance of San Francisco to need any reference to them here—already of no contemptible size, a few years will behold it a large and flourishing city. Yet although there is a Protestant minister here whose congregation af-forded him a liberal support, the Catholic congregation of the town, among whom there are some Americans of standing, have to divide their pastor with two other large parishes on the other side of the bay of San Francisco, and he has to spend a large portion of each month in the saddle. And, when the priest celebrates Mass in San Francisco, he does so at the Mission three miles from town (Mission Dolores) there being no chapel in the town, that, during the rainy season (and, in fact, during the whole year for the poor) it is a matter of difficulty to get to church when Mass is celebrated . . . (6)

St. Francis Church — 1849 . . .

But the future pastor of St. Francis Church (7), the aggressive Father Anthony Langlois, (1812-1892), (8) would not let the mat-ter rest in such a sorry state and as he writes in his journal:

It was evident already that it was to become a large city, the em-porium of a large trade, center of communication, etc., but no church, no religion, no means of starting it. People so busy for money and for settling

4

how they could make more. Many in passage only for a little while, and all strangers to each other . . .

Several acquaintances met together in a small meeting and five or six subscribed $200. each, found the lot where it is now St. Francis Church, obtained my consent and bought it for $5,000. We went immediately to prepare the little house on it for a chapel.

The first committeemen were P. H. Burnett, Mr. Sherbrook, Mr. Howard, Major Hardy, Mr. H. Davis, and Mr. Brouillet . . . the building was constructed to hold as many persons as possible, care being taken to avoid anything that might divide or narrow it. Its walls and ceilings were covered with this white cloth. Some ladies adorned its little altar. Afterwards we took up our abode in the attic, viz., Father Brouillet, Father Langlois . . . Religion now began to be practiced a little in spite of all the natural obstacles thrown in its way by the pursuit of gold, gold, of which all had come in search from every part of the globe; in spite, moreover, of the drawbacks of uncertain employment, of various inconveniences, of the interminglings of people, strangers to one another, and this in tents for a considerable number; in spite of the temptations of barrooms and saloons on every hand for the multitude that frequented them, to amuse themselves, drink and spend their time; in spite of the smallness of what was at once church and residence, and the poorness of its exterior; all taken in conjunction with the shortcomings of its curate (Father Langlois himself) who was called upon to speak English, Spanish, and French in the same sermon, that he might be understood by all; as well as the lack of time needed to go and invite Catholic households to church and let them know that it was possible for a person to save his soul in San Francisco. (9)

Thus ended the pastoral days of Spanish California. San Francisco now had an "American" Catholic Church even if the pastor had to preach in three languages. The vine which had been planted and watered by the blood of Franciscan martyrs could not flourish in the soil made sterile by Mexican opposition and oppression. But the mixture of fresh Catholic immigrant strength and religious liberty under the Constitution of the United States gave promise of luxuriant future growth. A small group of Catholics would soon welcome, at St. Francis of Assisi Church, San Francisco, a naturalized citizen of the United States, Joseph Sadoc Alemany, (10) then Bishop of Monterey, and later first Archbishop of the Archdiocese of San Francisco. (11)

5

Old St. Mary's Church
Before the 1906 Earthquake
The building on the right is
the Archbishop's Residence

PART ONE

THE BISHOP WHO WAS A BUILDER

Joseph Sadoc Alemany (1814-1888)

First Bishop of Monterey (1850-1853)

First Archbishop of San Francisco (1853-1884)

The Bishop Comes . . .

In attempting to recapture the colorful San Francisco that was, writers have seized upon men rather than places to sketch their story. Perhaps one of the most colorful of these men was the familiar figure known and humorously addressed by thousands as Emperor Norton the First (1819-1880). (12) Oftentimes in recounting the story of old San Francisco his death has been used to mark the end of one of the city's most colorful eras. On January 8, 1880, on California Street at Grant Avenue, Emperor Norton the First, bedecked in his royal blue uniform lavish with gilt epulets and brass braid suddenly slumped to the pavement. It was early in the evening, and as the twilight quickly deepened into darkness the large stone building before which he lay cast its darkening shadow over the limp figure like a funeral pall. The story of this colorful early San Franciscan has been told and retold, (13) and yet, strangely enough few have caught the significance of where he died—literally in the shadow of San Francisco history. For the building before which he died breathes San Francisco history to all who can read the past in the aging stone and worn red brick that is Old St. Mary's, San Francisco's first Cathedral.

Our story does not begin with the half-demented Norton, nor even does it begin with the Cathedral standing forth in the morning sun so new the mortar between its bricks had not yet set. Rather, our story goes back to the man who envisoned a great Church in California and built a great Cathedral as proof of his faith in the growth that he knew must come to the Church in California. That man was Joseph Sadoc Alemany, first Archbishop of San Francisco.

After the 1906 Earthquake Fire

Need of a Bishop . . .

God in His Wisdom raises up great men in times of great need. In 1849-1850, California was desperately in need of such a man and pastor as Bishop Joseph Sadoc Alemany. In virtue of the Treaty of Guadalupe Hidalgo (1848) California had passed out of the avaracious and inefficient hands of the *"paisanos"* and was soon to enjoy an organized government of its own, subject only to the Central Government of Washington. (14) This was a government of English speaking Americans largely. The Catholic Church in California was as yet suffragan to the Archdiocese of Mexico City. Since the death of Bishop Garcia Diego on April 30, 1846, this diocese of Both Californias had been entrusted to Father Gonzales Rubio, as Governor of the Mitre, (1804-1875). (15) Although he attempted to govern wisely and zealously, he was hindered both by the attachment of his diocese to the jurisdiction of the Archdiocese of Mexico City and also because he lacked episcopal powers. Although he could administer the Sacrament of Confirmation, (16) he could not ordain priests, nor could he bless the Holy Oils which at this time were furnished by the Bishop of Valparaiso, Chile, or from the Sandwich Islands (Hawaiian Islands of today). This coupled with the tremendous increase in population and the urgent demand for an English speaking Bishop made it vitally necessary that a bishop be furnished, preferably from the clergy of the United States, who would be familiar with the problems of the new immigrants to California.

Letters from prominent Catholics, who were in California at this time had acquainted the bishops of the United States with the situation as it existed in California. The bishops added their own voice to these appeals to Rome for a Catholic Bishop for California. An imposter representing himself as a Papal Nuncio with the power to arrange all ecclesiastical matters had visited California and after obtaining small sums had fled. (17) This news was brought to the attention of Rome and showed the necessity of some immediate action. On November 20, 1849, the Pope selected the Rev. Charles Pius Montgomery, O.P., (1806-1860), who, earlier, as provincial of the Dominicans, had represented them at the Fourth Provincial Council of Baltimore, May 1840. Father Montgomery pleaded poor health and was excused from taking up the arduous duties of the episcopate by the Pope. (18) At this time Rev. Joseph Sadoc Alemany, who had succeeded Father Montgomery as Provincial of

7

the Dominicans, was representing the American Province at the General Chapter of the Order then being held in Rome. He was offered the position of Bishop of California but likewise did not wish to take up the heavy burden. Nothing was farther from the wishes of this Dominican Friar than to assume the episcopal dignity, but obedient to the wishes of the Pope and knowing something, at least, of the struggle of Bishop Diego, he accepted the appointment as Bishop of Monterey, May 31, 1850, and was consecrated as the new bishop of that See by Cardinal Franzoni in the Church of San Carlo at Rome on June 30, 1850. (19)

Thus it was that the Church of California received a man who was an American Citizen and was familiar with the problems of the immigrants coming to California from the United States and at the same time by heritage and language was sympathetic toward those in California who spoke the Spanish language. And although Bishop Alemany was well aware of the heavy burden that he was taking up in California, still he did not tarry along the way. The poverty and destitution of the Church of California was well known. Bishop Alemany wisely stopped on his journey to his new diocese in Spain, France, and Ireland to solicit church goods, and priests and sisters were asked to volunteer to come to California and help with the great task of transforming a chaotic melange into the well organized archdiocese which he offered to his successor, Archbishop Riordan, (1841-1914) (20) on December 28, 1884.

Arrival in San Francisco . . .

The respectable citizens of the little town of San Francisco had retired to their homes on the evening of December 6, 1850. The rowdy element of this city swelled by the discovery of gold was only settling down to the raucous pleasures of Portsmouth Square when the steamer Columbus slipped quietly through the Golden Gate and dropped anchor in the stream to await the coming of day. On board were ninety-five passengers who had come to San Francisco for a multitude of reasons. But of the varied passenger list one name marked the beginning of a new era for California. For "Rev. Joseph Alemany, in company with Rt. Rev. Joseph Vilarassa," had arrived in San Francisco at 11 P. M., December 6, 1850. (21) Although Bishop Alemany had been assigned to California and raised to the plentitude of the priesthood on June 30, 1850, this

8

fact was not yet known to the clergy of California. With the coming of day, however, San Francisco knew that their long sought for shepherd of the flock had arrived. Right Rev. Joseph Alemany was the new Bishop of California, under American rule, and the era of Mexican governmental restriction and interference in church matters was at an end.

At first Father Langlois, the pastor of St. Francis Church, which was the only Catholic Church in the city of San Francisco since Mission Dolores, three miles away, was far beyond the town as it existed at that time, welcomed Bishop Alemany with certain reservations. A recent "Papal Nuncio" and other imposters had led Father Langlois to be wary of such visitors. But Bishop Alemany presented his credentials and Father Langlois recognized them to be genuine and now knew the long awaited Bishop had arrived. An immediate reception was hastily organized and on December 10, 1850, the leading Catholic citizens welcomed their new Bishop. On that evening in the little frame church of St. Francis a committee of welcome, composed of Messrs. John A. McGlynn, Hugh O'Donnell, P. Moffat O'Brien, M.D., Charles D. Carter, George O'Doherty, Thomas Jefferson Smith, Dennis McCarthy, and R. F. Ryan, presented Bishop Alemany with a purse of $1,350 (22) and read the following address of welcome:

To the Right Rev. Joseph Alemany,
Bishop of California
Right Rev. Sir:

The Catholics of San Francisco, in public meeting assembled, feel bound to express our gratitude to Almighty God for the signal favor He has conferred upon us, in sending an exalted teacher to govern and instruct this Church in this part of the world. As Your spiritual children in Christ, we rejoice to meet You as our Father and Prelate, and we bid You a hearty welcome to this land.

The distinguished position to which you had been already raised in the Church, the estimation in which You were held by the Hierarchy of the United States, who nominated You to the Holy See for our Bishop, and the reputation You have long enjoyed for those virtues and qualifications befitting an ecclesiastical dignitary, give us the most assured confidence that you are worthy of the Episcopacy, and that Your career among us will furnish an exemplification of the character described by the inspired writers. "Behold a great priest who in his time pleased God

9

and was found just, and in the time of wrath was made a reconciliator."

We feel deeply sensible to the exertions You have made to secure for us the services of a zealous and devoted Priesthood from Spain, France, Ireland, and the United States and we are sure the whole community will participate in the pleasure it has afforded us to learn that You also have taken measures to enlist in the cause of Religion here, the Sisters of Charity—those self-sacrificing handmaids of Christ, who are everywhere found ministering angels to suffering humanity.

To this welcome Bishop Alemany responded in English, French and Spanish not as a vain display of his command of languages but as a necessary means of reaching the various groups which still preserved their individual languages. (23)

Bishop Alemany's Early Days . . .

On December 14, 1850, Bishop Alemany left for Santa Barbara to show his Bulls of Consecration to the Administrator, Gonzalez Rubio and to take formal possession of his diocese. On Christmas Day, Bishop Alemany reached Santa Barbara and formally took possession of the Diocese of Both Californias. Bishop Alemany remained at Santa Barbara for several weeks and on the fourth of February established himself at Monterey, the seat of his diocese as fixed by Rome. Here in the pueblo church of San Carlos, Monterey, Bishop Alemany established his pro-Cathedral. (24) This church remained his pro-Cathedral until July 9, 1853, when he transferred his residence to San Francisco. The former episcopal seat of the diocese, Monterey, had remained a Spanish town largely undisturbed by the tremendous influx of immigrants in search of life in the land of gold. If Bishop Alemany were to properly care for the spiritual needs of these people, he must of necessity establish the episcopal residence where these new immigrants could more readily receive his attention and ministrations. Therefore, he transferred his residence to San Francisco and established diocesan headquarters at St. Francis Church, in that city.

Before Bishop Alemany could turn his thoughts to the building of a new cathedral, however, there was more pressing business that must be given his personal attention. His first year in the new diocese was spent in episcopal visitations and a vigorous attempt to set the Church in California upon a strong foundation. In 1852 he prepared to attend the First Plenary Council of the Bishops of the

10

United States in Baltimore. On April 1, 1852, he appointed Father Gonzalez Rubio his vicar general for the whole diocese and his administrator during his absence. Because of the size of the diocese and the distances involved, he appointed, subject to Father Rubio's jurisdiction, Rev. F. J. Llebaria (1814-?) as vicar general of the northern part of California. (25)

After attending the Council of Baltimore, Bishop Alemany returned by way of Mexico City where he attempted to reach some understanding with the Mexican Government concerning the payments of the Pious Fund to the Church in California which were far in arrears. After much subterfuge and dilatory tactics, the Government of Mexico finally admitted it did not intend to live up to the agreement which had been reached when the Government of Mexico confiscated the Pious Fund. This matter would not be settled until November 11, 1875, when Sir Edward Thornton, serving as Umpire in the Mixed Commission between the United States and Mexico, decided in favor of the Bishop in the case of the Pious Fund. Bishop Alemany returned to this Diocese in the first week of November, 1852. (26)

Bishop Alemany Is Made An Archbishop . . .

When Bishop Alemany returned to San Francisco in November, 1852, it was evident to him that he could not satisfactorily care for the needs of his flock as long as he must traverse the Pacific Coast from Oregon to Mexico, and be responsible for the care of souls living as far inland as the boundaries of Kansas and Nebraska. A division of the diocese was necessary, and, inasmuch as the Americans unlike the "Californios" were willing to support their Hierarchy, Rome, on July 29, 1853, appointed Bishop Alemany the first Ordinary of the newly erected Archdiocese of San Francisco, and Bishop Amat (1811-1878) the new Bishop of Monterey and Los Angeles as suffragan bishop to Archbishop Alemany. (27) But twelve days before this event took place in Rome, Bishop Alemany alert to the needs of his times had laid the cornerstone of his new Cathedral in San Francisco. The days of frame churches serving as temporary or pro-Cathedrals was at an end. Archbishop Alemany was building his great new Cathedral.

The Bishop Builds . . .

This was not the first cathedral contemplated by a prelate in

11

California. Bishop Garcia Diego y Moreno had also dreamed of a great stone church which would announce to the whole world the strength of Catholicism in California. But, like the promised support of the Catholic Church by the "Californios," his dream of a cathedral was never realized. When Bishop Diego came to Santa Barbara at the invitation of the inhabitants he planned a beautiful cathedral. But his dreams of a cathedral lasted only long enough to see the stones brought for the foundation. Then he realized the assistance promised by the Mexican government was only an empty promise and for long years the stones for the foundation of the first cathedral in California lay as they were dumped except for the overgrowth of weeds. (28)

The Site for the Cathedral . . .

The story of the actual building of the Cathedral of St. Mary's begins with the selection of a site. One of the early pioneers, John Sullivan, (29) was the generous donor of the land where St. Mary's, the first Cathedral of San Francisco, was built. When Bishop Alemany announced his plans for the building of a cathedral, John Sullivan came forward and offered the site upon which the building was built. Although some criticized the Bishop for erecting his Cathedral so far from the heart of the city, which at this time was grouped around Portsmouth Plaza, nevertheless, the site was on a prominent location and a valuable piece of property. The Bishop accepted this site and planned to build.

When Father Herbert Vaughan (1832-1903), the future Cardinal Archbishop of Westminster, visited California in the early months of 1864, he described the building of the Cathedral as follows:

When after 1849, the rush to the diggings took place, and all men were suffering from "The Gold Fever" and "silver on the brain," spending their money in wholesale gambling, making fortunes one week and losing them the next, and every man's head seemed to be turned by the helter-skelter excitement, the Catholic Church in her calm majesty was growing up in the midst of the turmoil and occupying her position as the city on the mountain and the light shining before men. The zeal of the Archbishop and clergy and faithful Irish knew no limits; churches sprang up in the conspicuous ninences of the city of San Francisco and in the principal thoroughfares. And the vast assemblage of men, who had come together from all parts, without religion or God in their hearts began to see that

12

they were in the presence of the Catholic Church and the shadow of the Catholic crosses and towers had fallen upon them. As soon as the Holy See gave to San Francisco an Archbishop the zealous sons of St. Patrick determined to build him a Cathedral. The wages of the common hodman were two pounds, ten shillings a day; nevertheless while the Catholic with one hand worked or scrambled for wealth, with the other he freely gave to that which is always dearest to his heart. The deep foundations of the Cathedral were sunk, the walls arose, its massive time keeping tower crowned the city, its solemn services were inaugurated. It was the result of fabulous sums of money, and of heroic devotedness on the part of pastors and people. (30)

A decade had brought tremendous change to California. Had Father Vaughan visited California during 1852 and 1853, he might not have found the "zealous sons of St. Patrick" so determined to build a Cathedral for their Archbishop. During these years, California was undergoing a period of depression, business failures, and unemployment. The then Bishop Alemany had to struggle against heavy odds to build his Cathedral.

On June 1, 1853, Bishop Alemany issued the following Pastoral Letter:

"To the Catholics of San Francisco, and the Diocese generally, Health and Holy Zeal.

Dearly Beloved Brethren:

In the early part of 1850, the Catholics of San Francisco, trusting more in the activity of their faith than in the strength of their number, undertook to build a frame church 40 by 75 feet on the lot purchased by them on Vallejo Street. The increase of the city and the growth of the congregation soon required the erection of another church, which was built in the summer of 1851, in the southern part of the city . . . and which has since become too small to accomodate that congregation. This being also the case with the church on Vallejo Street, a gallery was constructed in it, and last winter the building was considerably enlarged; but notwithstanding the additional space thus obtained, it is still found too small. It is not capable of accommodating the congregation who are in regular attendance there every Sunday—much less the numbers who come to behold the solemnity of our ceremonies, and to hear our doctrines explained.

It seems that this city has had the singular privilege of attaining, immediately after its foundation, a growth which in other large cities was

13

the work of successive generations. San Francisco is great in a commercial point of view, in population, and in the strength of its resources. And shall we not endeavor to make religion keep pace with all this progress? Every intelligent mind perceives that the greatest benefit that can be bestowed on our community is the holy influence of religion. The majesty of the God whom we adore demands that His holy temples should be, if not as rich as he deserves, at least the best we can make them. The faithful of all nations have always raised magnificent temples to the glory of God— the lasting monuments of their piety.

Urged by the insufficiency of church accommodation caused by the rapid increase of our population, we should consider ourselves greatly negligent in our duty, if we did not undertake to build another church of larger dimensions.

It was with this view that a lot was purchased in the northeast corner of California and Dupont Streets, (3) and a chaste and elegant design in the gothic style of architecture has been prepared by Messrs. Craine and England, Architects, for the contemplated St. Mary's Church. It is but obvious that the new church should be capacious enough to meet the increasing wants of the people; it is prudent to make the building solid and lasting, so as to avoid the repetition of the expense; it is fit to give some elegance to the edifice, since the improved style of buildings in the city demanded it; and finally, it is just that we should raise a church as magnificent as our means will allow, since we are building a house not for men, but for God.

We, therefore, earnestly appeal to the piety of every Catholic in California, and particularly to those in the city; we exhort you all to pay a tribute to Almighty God by a generous offering; we entreat you to enable us with your generous subscriptions to build St. Mary's Church. We are confident that God through His invisible hand will not fail to reward the pious giver.

The grace of our Lord Jesus Christ be with all of you."

Joseph S. Alemany
Bishop of Monterey, California
San Francisco, Calif., June 1st, 1853. (32)

Financing the Cathedral . . .

But Bishop Alemany was not content to wait until the generous Catholic brought his contribution for the new church. Because Bishop Alemany felt the proposed Cathedral was essential to the

14

growth of the Church he willingly went from door to door for donations to build his new Cathedral. This zeal and humility is described as follows:

He (Father Gallagher) was then appointed pastor of the flourishing parish of St. Francis in this city, where he enlarged and otherwise improved the church, and just as he concluded this labor of love, Archbishop Alemany requested his services to assist in the erection of the contemplated new Cathedral. Father Gallagher (33) gladly accepted the honorable position and in conjunction with his beloved Archbishop, solicited day after day, through sunshine and storm, along the streets, and wharves, and alleys, and out in the sand hills of the scattered city, until they could say with gratified hearts, "Consummatum est—it is completed." And thus St. Mary's Cathedral was built through the benevolence of the pioneers of this city and the persevering efforts of the pioneer Archbishop and his faithful ally—Father Hugh P. Gallagher. (34)

Having received the site, Bishop Alemany immediately proceeded with the building of the new Cathedral. The architects were two prominent San Franciscans of the time, William Craine and John England. The general plan of the church was to be Gothic in design modified to the physical requirements of the site. Originally it had been planned to erect a large steeple on the church but during the course of construction this was modified and the steeple was never erected. In the artist's sketch which accompanies this work the tower is shown as contemplated. In the picture taken of the church in 1856, the steel framework that was to have strengthened the tower is shown. Later this was removed when it was decided, because of the danger of earthquake, not to erect the steeple.

On July 17, 1853, the foundation had progressed sufficiently so that the ceremony of the laying of the cornerstone could be carried out. The event is fully described in the *San Francisco Daily Herald* on the following day, July 18, 1853:

The imposing ceremonies of the laying of the cornerstone of this church, situated on the northeast corner of California and Dupont streets, took place yesterday.

At eleven o'clock the spectators had assembled in large numbers, filling the space within the foundation walls, and the adjoining streets and everyone seemed eager to witness the approaching ceremonies.

At twelve o'clock the solemn music of a band, engaged for the occasion, announced the approach of the Right Reverend Bishop, who

15

was accompanied by a suite of several officiating clergy robed in the vestments of their sacred offices and preceeded by the bearer of the chalice (Sic) containing the holy water. The officiating clergymen assembled around the stone with the imposing solemnity and dignity peculiar to the service of the Catholic Church. The treasure and memorials prepared for the occasion were then deposited in the stone which was sanctified by the sprinkling of the holy water and the mark of the cross.

The trowel used by the Bishop in the performance of the ceremony was of solid silver of an ordinary size with a wooden handle and bore the following inscription:

St. Mary's Church

San Francisco, California

Joseph S. Alemany, Bishop

July 17, 1853

Crane (Sic) and England Architects

The Bishop, proceeded by the ecclesiastical cortege, then slowly traversed the foundation of the building casting around him the holy water whilst the procession chanted the solemn service of the Church. Returning to the corner, the ceremony of laying the stone was concluded by the Bishop.

The Rev. Father Gallagher then addressed the assemblage, in explanation of the ceremony, and read the following paper which is a translation of the original in Latin, deposited in the stone:

May it be for the honor of the Church of Christ,

For the weal of the commonwealth,

And for the benefit of the Christian People,

That the Corner Stone of this New Temple

Dedicated to the Almighty God

Under the title of St. Mary, Ever Virgin, and

Conceived Without Sin,

Is blessed and laid on California Street,

In the City of San Francisco,

In the presence of the assembled people

With solemn rites and ceremonies—

Assisting, the Reverend Clergymen, John Francis Liebaria (Sic), Vicar General, Eugene O'Connell, Superior of the Seminary, Hugh P. Gallagher, Pastor of St. Mary's, Anthony Jimeno, Missionary of the College of San Fernando, Flavian Fontain (Sic) Pastor of the Mission of San Francisco, and three seminarians.

16

By the Illustrious and Right Reverend Prelate,
Joseph Sadoc, Bishop of Monterey,
At 11 o'clock A.M., on the 17th day of July
In the year of grace, 1853,
And of American Independence the 78th
While seated in the chair of St. Peter
Pope Pius the Ninth.
President of the United States—Franklin Pierce:
Governor of the State of California—John Bigler.
Mayor of the City of San Francisco—Chas. J. Brenham.
Architects: William Crane (Sic) and Thomas England.

The articles were deposited in a sealed bottle, and consisted of the following: The above explanatory remarks, copy of each of the city papers; Catholic Almanac; Trask's Geological Report; Proceedings of the First National Council of Baltimore; specimens of different religious medals and various coins and a rosary.

This part of the ceremony having been concluded the same reverend gentleman addressed the audience extemporaneously taking as his text: "The stone which I have set up shall be called the House of God."

Gen. XXXIII, 22.

"In perusing ecclesiastical intelligence of today," said the speaker, "in reading of the triumphs of faith and grace—the propagation of the Church—the extension and consolidation of Christ's Kingdom on earth— we are not only pleased, but we gather even strength and consolation from these tidings. When the mercy of God comes to our own threshold, that we have been, in a word appointed the builders of God's house —who shall gainsay us if we should raise up our voices and our hearts and express our gratitude and praise our Lord of Hosts?"

Having spoken of the liturgy in Latin, the ornaments of the Bishop, the robes of his sacred office, the insignia of his deserved dignity, the speaker remarked, that (Sic) on these venerated emblems, the crowd, unlearned in their own past history, might be puzzled with astonishment; but they announce the presence of an authority holier and more ancient than that of Emperors, Kings, and Commoners.

"We did not come today," he exclaimed, "to suffer for the cherished faith, but to see a spot of God's own earth consecrated to him back again; to set up a stone for a title, as did Jacob of yore; to mark the spot where another tent was to be pitched in the camp of Israel, another altar dedicated to the Lord of Hosts."

17

He remarked on the changed conditions of the place. But a few years since it was a dreary waste of barren sand, whose monotony was only broken by the sea bird's scream.

The orator then appealed to the brethren to persevere—to proceed with courage and zeal. "You have," he said, "an evidence in your Chief of God's mercy. Look to him as a guarantee of success. Persevere and let the prayers of all be poured forth to speed the good work." With an earnest appeal and benediction the speaker concluded.

During the concluding remarks a collection was taken up to advance the work, after which a discourse was delivered in French, and also in Spanish, by the Very Rev. John Francis Liebaria (Sic); Vicar General of the Diocese. (35)

From Corner Stone To Dedication . . .

From July 17, 1853, until the dedication of the Cathedral on December 25, 1854, the work progressed slowly. The principal difficulty was to obtain the necessary building materials. As yet the local building industry had not progressed to the point where it could supply its own materials. The stone for the foundation was quarried and cut in China and shipped to be assembled for the foundation according to a prefabrication plan. The brick for the walls was brought from New England around the Horn in sailing ships. The lumber used in the construction was purchased at the inflated price of $325 per thousand feet. Despite the draining off of skilled labor to the gold fields and the shortage of material the work progressed until late in December, 1854, the announcement of the proposed dedication was made.

Over a year prior to the dedication, in November, 1853, a parish fair was held for the purpose of aiding the erection of St. Mary's Cathedral. This fair netted more than seven thousand dollars for the building fund. The California correspondent of the *New York Freeman's Journal* describes the event as follows:

It is spoken of by all as having been one of the grandest affairs of the kind that has yet been witnessed in California. The ladies shall deserve great credit for their zeal and liberality, and the result of their labors must be gratifying to themselves as it is to the Catholics of California generally. (36)

Shortly after this fair the Church Debt Society was established whereby wealthy members of the parish undertook to pay regularly into a fund to retire the Cathedral building debt.

As a further means of raising current revenue the pews of the new Cathedral were rented. To attract notice to the proposed sale of pews, the *Daily Alta California* carried the following item:

CATHEDRAL OF ST. MARY'S

As this magnificent edifice will be opened for Divine Service on Monday next, (Christmas Day) the pews will be disposed of by auction on Saturday, the 23rd instant, at 11 o'clock A.M., at which time all interested are invited to attend at the church, corner of California and Dupont Streets. (37)

The sale of pews was entirely successful and, although most of the pews were rented for the year for the sum of $80 to $100, a few choice pews were rented by the generous pioneers for sums up to $175.

The Dedication of the Cathedral

The great day had finally arrived. Although it was already early evening the sound of the carpenter's hammers still resounded through the great bare Cathedral on Christmas Eve, December 24, 1854. Almost devoid of all ornamentation, the great edifice was to be dedicated (38) on one of the greatest feast days of the year, at Midnight Mass, Christmas Day, December 25, 1854.

As the hour appointed for the ceremonies approached, the work of putting in the pews was rushed at a feverish pace. The carpenters did not finish their work until 9 o'clock and already a great throng was milling around the doors eager to enter their Cathedral and attend Midnight Mass. (39) Not only were Catholics eager to enter but a large number of persons of other religious beliefs desired to commemorate the Birth of Christ in the magnificent new structure. The dedication of the new Cathedral so caught the fancy of the whole city that long before the ceremonies were to begin the structure was filled far beyond its capacity and an immense throng stood on the sidewalks of California and Dupont Streets outside the Cathedral.

Archbishop Alemany wrote to his mother, December 27, 1854, describing the great crowd that came to the dedication:

. . . The Cathedral of which I sent you the plan is large, not so large as that of Vich, and all were surprised to see it as full as an egg. One hour before the ceremony the people were hurrying to the bell tower and to the galleries which at present have nothing but the beams . . . I do not

remember having seen a church more crowded, and they told me that more than a thousand people had to turn back not being able to enter. (40)

In recalling the event some years later, the Reverend John F. Harrington, who acted as Master of Ceremonies at the Midnight Mass, remarked that the Church was crowded to its utmost capacity and that he "never saw it so crowded since." (41)

The Daily California Chronicle, published in San Francisco, in the yet short American Period history of San Francisco. The paper sent one of its staff to secure an eye-witness account of the event. Unfortunately he did not secure the story he wished. He reported his impressions of the event as follows:

Our reporter soon contrived to force his way through a dense mass of troubled and cursing (Sic) humanity, but soon he, with hundreds more, was too glad to escape from the terrible pressure within. Many ladies who had ventured inside of the passage ran considerable risk of being trampled upon. (42)

But it must not be understood that the Midnight Mass and dedication of the Cathedral was witnessed by a "cursing" mob. The pews had been placed in the center of the Cathedral and the entire congregation within the walls devoutly attended. Nor must it be thought that the ceremonies lacked for any dignity. The Mass of the occasion was the Solemn Pontifical Mass celebrated by Archbishop Alemany, himself. The music for the occasion was Hayden's celebrated "No. 3," and though unadorned the walls of St. Mary's reverberated to the swell of music as majestic as could be heard in any Cathedral of Europe. The solemn ceremonies of the Church were carried out in their full dignity and splendor. Whatever crowding or crushing of people there was, limited itself to the curious thronging in the doorways seeking to witness the great event.

The only note that was lacking was the chiming of the Cathedral bells. The music of the Mass was furnished by a full orchestra unaccompanied by the organ which was not installed until 1856. The Cathedral bell was hung and rung out for the first time on June 18, 1855. But the people of San Francisco did not need a church bell to remind them that they had a Cathedral. Standing on the heights looking down over their city was the largest structure yet erected in San Francisco. They lived, worked, and were constantly reminded of their obligations as a Christian people by the mighty red brick structure which in the morning reflected on them the warm rays of the rising sun, and in the evening cast its shadow over them as it stood silhouetted in the red glow of sunset. As the first Archbishop of San Francisco watched his flock file out of the new Cathedral Christmas morning, 1854, he might well have thought, "Surely, now Christ is born in this house raised for His Glory—the most magnificent structure among all the pursuits of men in this City of San Francisco."

On April 18, 1868, fourteen years after the Cathedral was completed, a meeting was held to which the prominent Catholics of the city were invited for the purposes of reducing the outstanding debt which remained upon the Cathedral. Because there is so much interest concerning the financing and cost of building the Cathedral we quote *The Monitor* in full:

It gives us as it will give many of our readers much satisfaction to learn that measures are about to be adopted to relieve St. Mary's Cathedral of a portion of its debt, and make some desirable improvements on the interior of the sacred edifice. On the evening of Monday, April 13, (1868) a respectable representation of the leading Catholic gentlemen of this city, assembled at the invitation of the Archbishop, at the Cathedral, to hear a statement of the temporal administration and financial condition of the church, and devise means of lightening its burden and render it more worthy of its character as the chief church of the diocese.

From the statement read to the meeting by the Archbishop it appeared that the total cost of St. Mary's Cathedral to the 1st of January, 1860, was about $175,000 and the indebtedness at the date $47,000. However large these amounts may appear to a person unacquainted with the enormous price of material and labor at the time the Cathedral was built, the Archbishop explained that all contracts were invariably given to the lowest responsible bidders and only after consultation with some of the leading members of the congregation. Since the 1st of January, 1860, an increase of the debt has been inevitable. With the diffusion of population from the old center of the city, the revenue of the Cathedral has necessarily decreased, while some changes and improvements have had to be made on and around the church. The old residence of the Archbishop and clergy on Dupont Street, after having long been a surprise to strangers, and an inconvenience to its occupants, has been at last abandoned and the new house with its baptistry between it and the

21

church erected at a cost of $35,000. Besides the roof of the Cathedral has been renewed and the front simply yet sufficiently adorned with stone steps and an iron railing, entailing an additional expense of about $8,500. A considerable amount has been paid also for sewering and paving the streets adjoining the Cathedral and a large sum is interest.

To meet all of these liabilities, $18,000 were collected by the Archbishop for his new residence and about $9,000 have been received from pew rents and other sources since 1860. The balance of the pew rent has been expended on the choir and school, while the Sunday collections have constituted the support of the Archbishop's house.

Having made the statement of the temporal administration and financial condition of St. Mary's Cathedral, the Archbishop proceeded to observe that he should have sooner availed himself of the generous promises made when the church was started, but he had wished to waive the claims of the Cathedral in favor of the many institutions of charity calling for public aid. Now, however, he thought the time had come to bring the necessities of St. Mary's Cathedral to the notice of its friends, especially as he was anxious to pay for and place behind the altar a magnificent painting of the Immaculate Conception executed by one of the most distinguished artists of Rome and probably already on its way to San Francisco.

John T. Doyle, (43) C. D. Carter, (44) and Major General Rosecrans, (45) and others addressed the meeting after the Archbishop, urging the propriety of prompt action to relieve, and as far as possible complete the chief church of the diocese, and it was unanimously resolved that an appeal should be made to the Catholic Body generally, and especially to the immediate congregation of St. Mary's Cathedral. (46)

Before leaving the story of the building of St. Mary's Cathedral, it is fitting that a few words be given concerning the generosity of the donor of the site, John Sullivan. As a mark of appreciation of the generosity of John Sullivan to the Catholic Church, his first wife, Catherine Sullivan, who died August 10, 1854, at the age of twenty-six years, was buried beneath the main altar of the Cathedral shortly before it was completed. Two other early Catholic pioneers were buried in crypts beneath the main altar: Father John Reardon, (?-1857), pastor of Placerville, and Ana Maria Robinson, daughter of Jose Maria Alfredo Robinson, who died February 11, 1860 at the age of twenty-two years. Robinson was an American who came to California during the Mexican period, became a Mexican citizen,

22

and took the name Alfredo. Today only the remains of Catherine Sullivan and Ana Robinson rest in individual crypts beneath the foundations of the main altar. The remains of Father Reardon have been transferred to the Roman Catholic Cemetery, Holy Cross, outside the city limits of San Francisco.

Besides his donation of the site of the Cathedral, John Sullivan contributed the following to the Catholic Church:

He joined with Mr. A. B. McCreery in a gift of five 50 vara lots to Calvary Cemetery. He donated to the Archbishop for St. Mary's College the block of six 50 vara lots on Larkin Street on which the Mechanics Pavilion was built. He donated $5,000 to the fund for the Presentation Convent erected on Powell and Lombard Streets. He gave the land on which the Church at Mountain View was built and paid for the cost of erecting this church. He built Old St. Patrick's Church, later the pro-Cathedral when moved to Eddy Street, and now used as a gymnasium for Holy Cross Parish. He donated $12,000 to the Presentation Convent on Taylor Street. He gave a like sum to Sacred Heart College. He always held that charity was its own reward and this was verified when in a moment of financial embarrassment, his building having been destroyed by fire in one of the frequent conflagrations of this city in the early '50's, the first man to come to his aid was Archbishop Alemany who said, "I can never forget the first $20 gold piece I received in San Francisco was from your dear wife. Here is $5,000; take it, build up your houses. Repay me when you can." (47)

23

St. Mary's after the 1906
Earthquake Fire

PART TWO

ST. MARY'S CATHEDRAL

THE CENTER OF CATHOLIC LIFE

HOIST THAT FLAG!

The Cathedral in the Civil War
Demonstrations of 1861

When William Craine and Thomas England sketched the plans for St. Mary's Cathedral, they provided for a solid stone foundation to withstand the earth shocks which might be expected in this region. But they did not visualize an even greater shock that would convulse California society. The Civil War, which pitted brother against brother and rent the Federal Union into two armed camps, reached bloody hands toward California in the Spring of 1861. Fortunately wisdom prevailed over emotion and violence was not necessary to hold California within the fold of the Union. But emotion ran high in the Spring of '61, and a man's loyalty to the Union had to be expressed in no uncertain terms. As the possibility of open conflict drew closer the demands for a clear declaration in favor of the Union reached almost panic proportions.

On May 10, 1861, the San Francisco *Daily Evening Bulletin* carried numerous notices by various firms advertising a patriotic demonstration on the next day in favor of the Union. On May 12, 1861, this paper carried the following account of the demonstration:

. . . at first there was scarcely breeze enough to part bunting and flagstaff. The sun came out never more brilliantly. The sky was unclouded. The air was clear, but from the heights the whole city looked as if it were wrapped in Union Flags. The three colors that tinted all the streets were red, white and blue. Stars displayed everywhere in clusters of 34, seemed to outnumber the stars in the sky of a clear night, and wherever there was not a star there was a stripe. There were flags on every flagstaff, and flagstaffs pretty nearly everywhere, that they could be made to stick. Flags filled the windows, were hung from balconies, strung across streets, bedecked the head gear of horses in harness, waved in the hands of all boys . . . From this central point in the city, in every direction, the streets

St. Mary's Basement Today. It was here in August 1856 that San Francisco evening schools had their beginning. They were made possible by the cooperation of Archbishop Alemany with the City's Board of Education.

were waving and brilliant with flags. The horses that galloped by were blanketed with flags—flags on the head gear, on the saddles, on the stirrups, and in the rider's hands. Wherever you could see a young one, he was sure to be doing duty as a flagstaff. The cloth that was devoted to displaying the Stars and Stripes would clothe a regiment. Take the city through, it was only to be measured by the acre. (48)

"Flagging" the Churches ...

Feeling was kept at a high pitch during the following weeks and reached its climax with the approach of July 4, 1861. On June 28, the patriotic fervor had reached even the churches of the city. The *Daily Evening Bulletin,* San Francisco, announced this incident in the following glowing terms:

By 10 o'clock this morning, there was a crowd of ladies and gentlemen . . . gathered on the corner of Dupont and California Streets, facing the First Congregational Church. There were men on the top of the church tower raising, by aid of a set of shears on the roof, a tall straight pole, its upper end a gilded globe, and just below the globe the block with a cord reeved to hoist thereon the Union Flag. It was full 10½ before the eastern lean could be got out of the pole, so that it knew no north, no south, no west, nor even east, but looked only one way—toward heaven —under whose particular and broad protection lies our country. At a quarter to 11, all was ready. The Rev. Mr. Lacey handled the ropes, and heaving away with a will, there went up the prettiest flag in all creation to wit: The Stars and Stripes done in bunting of just proportions and bright colors—up to the top of the staff, and then Mr. Lacey belayed, while the four corners of the crossing echoed with cheers for the flag. (49)

However, not all were in agreement with raising the Union banner over the various churches in the city. The First Baptist Church members held a meeting on June 27 to consider the "taste, propriety, and patriotism and Christianity of hoisting a flag on their church. All were not of one way of thinking at first; but finally it was thought best to do it. (50)

St. Mary's Cathedral, as the principal church of the city, was expected to make a strong demonstration for the Union. Whatever the basis of the statement, the *Daily Evening Bulletin,* San Francisco, a strong pro-Union paper, declared:

We have been told on excellent authority that St. Mary's Cathedral is soon to have a flag reared above it of such dimensions that you could wrap in it all the Secessionists that dare show their heads in San Francisco

25

as in a winding sheet, and still have enough left to proclaim with perfect clearness that the Catholic Church is right for the Union. (51)

The editor of the paper ends the article on "flagging" (52) the churches with the significant statement that, "The first church in town to raise a flag was the Rev. Dr. Anderson's Old School Presbyterian. Let the notable and honorable fact be known and remembered." (53) On the following day the *Daily Alta California* halted the rumors of the "flagging" of the Cathedral with the statement:

We are informed on good authority that the report to the effect that a flag will soon be raised on St. Mary's Cathedral is without foundation. No intention of the kind is entertained. (54)

The fever of seeing the Stars and Stripes floating on the breeze reached its height when on July 3, 1861, the *Daily Alta California*, (San Francisco), published the following notice:

At sunrise tomorrow, a new flag, forty-two feet long by twenty-nine feet broad, will be raised upon the new flag staff on the Plaza.

The question of "flagging" the churches became a very real issue and the debate grew stronger as the Fourth of July approached. The *Daily Evening Bulletin* (San Francisco), left no doubt in the reader's mind when it published the following statement:

Whether or not flags should be displayed over places of worship was a question of taste a few weeks ago. It may still be, in localities where there can be no question as to the loyalty of all the people; but where there are secessionists mingling with Loyalists, and public sentiment is in danger of being corrupted while good citizens pursue the bent of their business or inclinations, this is rescued from the domain of mere taste, and becomes a consideration of patriotism; for it behooves everyone, in such a time as this, to let every other one know where he stands on the great issue of the day. (55)

To encourage the practice of "flagging" the churches, the editorial remark is made that "the 4th is, and must ever be a busy day, but there are many Christian people who will enjoy turning into a church, over which floats the Union Flag, for an hour before the most boisterous demonstrations of the day are fairly begun." (56)

The Reverend Mr. David B. Cheney, (1820 - ?), (57) praised the "flagging" of the churches in the most patriotic terms. At the occasion of the flagging of Washington Street Baptist Church, he questioned "the taste and propriety, and whether it met the issue for us to float the banner of our Country over our houses of worship."

26

He eliminated any doubt in the mind of the crowd by hurling this challenge:

But if withholding so simple an act; if abstaining from the performance of an act which, at the worst, could only be a matter of taste, is in danger of being construed into aid and comfort for the enemies of our country, better that the church be painted all over without and within with flags. (58)

In a similar vein the *True Pacific Messenger*, (San Francisco), quoted by the *Daily Alta California*, (San Francisco), rises to the heights of poetic language in urging the "flagging" of the synagogues:

Hoist Your Flags—Ubi bene, ubi Patria (Sic). As yet none of our synagogues has raised the flag of our country. That flag, brethren, has given to the Israelite a free and independent home. Under its protection the Jew and Gentile enjoy the privilege to worship their Maker in any manner their creed demands. Life and property have ever been safe under its folds. Equal right as men, citizens, and religionists have followed wherever its glorious colors have spread. Hoist that flag over the roof of the house devoted to the service of that God, whom we must all implore to protect it against the frivolous hands that wantonly have been stretched out to tear it to fragments. When you pray let the ensign of the Union float over your heads and pray heaven that these stars may never wander from the glory of Liberty and Union! Hoist that flag! There is no other portion of the community more indebted to its rule and power than the Hebrew! Nor has any other more to lose by secession than the Israelites. Like unto times of old, let us patriotically gather around that banner of our tribe, and under its shadow move on to our mission. The government of freedom, Union and Independence that is the universal way of the God of Israel! Hoist that flag! (59)

The mania for "flagging," whether decorous or not, led persons to actions which certainly had little effect on the successful conclusion of the Civil War. On July 18, 1861, the *Daily Alta California*, (San Francisco), proudly reports:

Flag the Mountain Tops:

On Tuesday of this week Messrs. Peck, Fowler, Every, and other citizens of the upper part of Napa Valley raised a staff and American flag on the summit of Mt. Helena, at the head of the valley. Several ladies were present, having climbed to the highest peak of this grand old sentinel, which is nearly 4,000 feet above the level of the sea, to lend their

27

presence to the patriotic act of decorating the lofty summit with the national emblem.

The solid patriotism of Archbishop Alemany had never been questioned. Yet it is a tribute to his clear thinking, at a time when so many were carried away by every appeal of oratory, that he reserved the Cathedral for the purpose for which it was built. It was sufficient to acknowledge the Union as the legitimate government of the United States and positively declare allegiance to that legitimate government. If other denominations wished to raise the flag on their churches, they could express their patriotism in that manner. The present author has never read any word of criticism that was ever directed by the press at Archbishop Alemany for not doing likewise. People realized that the Archbishop professed equal respect for the flag and all it symbolized, even though he felt that it should not be placed on a building dedicated to the worship of God. (60)

Music in San Francisco's First Cathedral . . .

In 1854, frontier life in the Golden State was largely devoted to securing the necessities of life; yet in San Francisco, in that year, great music was being rendered by trained artists in San Francisco's principal religious edifice, St. Mary's Cathedral. On December 25, 1854, the music of the solemn Mass of dedication was Hayden's celebrated "No. 3." This music was accomplished by the use of a full orchestra in the choir loft. It was not until 1856 that the organ had arrived from the Atlantic Coast. On December 24, 1856, the San Francisco *Daily Evening Bulletin* reported:

HIGH MASS AT THE ROMAN CATHOLIC CATHEDRAL

We acknowledge receipt of an invitation to attend the rehearsal of Beethoven's Mass in C" to take place at the Cathedral at 3 P.M., this afternoon under the direction of Mr. R. Farald. Mass will be celebrated at the Cathedral tomorrow (Christmas) at half past five and eleven A.M.

Although this music was provided to add solemnity to the services of the church, it must not be thought that this music was limited solely to church services. In keeping with the character of the building and the wishes of the Church, it was only proper that profane music, that is, music of a purely secular nature, would be excluded from the programs given. However, invitations were extended to Catholics and non-Catholics to attend programs of sacred music given in the evening or at times when religious services were not being conducted. Often too, lectures given to raise funds for various purposes were rendered more attractive to non-Catholics by including a select number of musical works in the evening's program.

On September 8, 1861, Reverend Father Prendergast (61) was scheduled to preach a sermon in aid of the Cathedral School. Notice of this sermon was given in the *Daily Alta California*, (San Francisco), in which the editor included notice of the following attractive musical program:

A choice selection of sacred music will be performed. The Keyre (Sic) and Gloria of Mozart's Grand Mass, No. 12, will be given before the discourse. This Mass is his masterpiece. Vespers will be dispensed with; however, the clergy will enter the sanctuary at seven o'clock, so that all may be seated before a quarter past seven, at which time precisely the first piece of music will be commenced. After the sermon, selections from Hayden's Mass No. 6, will be performed. The usual efficient choir of the Cathedral will be aided by a large number of our most talented vocalists, including Miss Louisa Frances O'Keefe, who will sing a solo in Mozart's Mass preceeding the delivery of the sermon. (62)

This policy of providing selections from the best sacred music as part of the religious and educational program of the Cathedral continued in the life of the Cathedral. In December, 1885, the organ of St. Mary's Church was enlarged by the addition of a sub-bass, at a cost of about $700 to make it fit for rendering adequately the sonorous strains of such masterpieces as Mozart's Grand Mass, No. 12. (63)

Oftentimes recitals of sacred music were given in the Cathedral for those who appreciated great music. To these concerts of sacred music popular artists who might be present in San Francisco often lent their talents as the announcement in *The Monitor* (San Francisco) indicated:

Those lovers of true music who will be so fortunate as to attend the next organ concert in the Cathedral, will enjoy a rare treat. The charming cantatrice, "Madame de la Motte," has consented to add to the attraction of the occasion by giving the audience a specimen of her rare quality of voice, and superior method of vocalization. She is no new candidate for fame, no novice, or mere debutante. Her singing has won for her renown, and enthusiastic admiration from the most fastidious audiences in Europe and America, and now that she gives the tribute of her rich voice to the

29

cause of religion, we are sure that her kindness will be thoroughly appreciated by all who will listen to her melodious notes, on Wednesday, October 29, (1890). (64)

From the few citations quoted it can be seen that the Cathedral of St. Mary's was one of the earliest centers of San Francisco for great music. From the very beginning it was the policy of the responsible authorities to bring to the Cathedral great sacred music performed in a manner destined to bring respect to the services of the Church and enjoyment of the great music which complement these services.

St. Mary's Cathedral School . . .

Bishop Joseph Alemany looked to the future when he constructed his Cathedral. The small number of Catholics in San Francisco on July 17, 1853, when the cornerstone was laid, could not be expected to bear the expenditure of $175,000 for a Cathedral Church. But the Prelate was looking to the future growth of the City of San Francisco and to the growth of the Catholic portion of that city. He realized that the Church cannot live for the day but must look to the growth that will surely come in the future. This confidence in the future is necessary for all builders, and Bishop Alemany was a great builder. That Bishop Alemany had confidence in the future growth of the Diocese of Monterey is clearly revealed in his efforts to bring Orders of Sisters to his diocese even before he had seen it himself. The primary purpose of bringing these Catholic Orders of Sisters to California was to provide education for the youth of his diocese.

In September, 1855, Archbishop Alemany opened a school in the Cathedral basement for the youth of the Cathedral parish. Within six weeks the school was functioning smoothly with an enrollment of 313 scholars. (65) The curriculum embraced a complete education divided into primary, intermediate, grammar, and high school, with optional courses in the classics, French and Spanish. (66) Although a schedule of tuition payable in advance was announced in the daily papers, it was announced in the same notice that those students who were unable to meet the cost of tuition would not be refused on such grounds. Thus in actual practice the schools were, for the poorer classes, free schools. (67)

Financing the Schools . . .

The problem of meeting the expenses incurred in providing

30

education free of cost to those who were unable to pay tuition was met primarily by collections for this purpose taken up at regular lectures, benefits and other entertainments given for the purpose of raising money for the continuation of the Cathedral School. To assist in this worthy cause so dear to the heart of the Archbishop, the most popular priests of the Archdiocese offered their services. The Rev. James Chrysostom Bouchard, S.J., (1823-1889), the most popular preacher among the Catholic clergy of San Francisco for many years, is mentioned as speaking for the benefit of the Cathedral school. That these public lectures were very successful is evident from the notices in *The Monitor,* (San Francisco), of 1867. Advance notice was given on March 20, 1867, as follows:

On Wednesday, the 31 inst., at 7½ o'clock, a lecture will be delivered by Rev. Father Bouchard in St. Mary's Cathedral, in aid of St. Mary's School. The subject will be "The Catholic Church and Common Sense." We are sure those who attend will be more than pleased, and those who will not, will miss a rare intellectual treat. Tickets may be had of the sexton of the Cathedral or at any of the Catholic book stores. (68)

This was followed in the next issue by another advance notice so that the Catholic population of the city were well aware of the event. In the issue of March 27, 1867, the public is urged to attend in even stronger terms than the preceding week:

Rev. Father Buchard's (Sic) Lecture—This eloquent divine will give a lecture in St. Mary's Cathedral next Wednesday evening on "The Catholic Church and Common Sense," the proceeds to be devoted to St. Mary's School . . . the lecture he is about to treat his audience to (never before delivered in San Francisco)—is said to be his best; and the object being one that commends itself to every good citizen, we hope to see the Cathedral filled on Wednesday evening to its utmost capacity. Some of the best musical talent in the city has been engaged for the occasion and will discourse choice arias. (69)

Evidently Reverend Father Bouchard was popular with the people of San Francisco because on April 3, 1867, *The Monitor,* (San Francisco), carried this account of the lecture:

St. Mary's Cathedral was crowded to its utmost capacity on Wednesday evening to hear the Rev. Father Buchard's (Sic) lecture on "The Catholic Church and Common Sense." Before the lecturer made his appearance in the pulpit, the choir, composed of the leading artists of the city, render-

31

ed some of the most select pieces. The reverend lecturer ascended the pulpit at about 8 o'clock. (70)

Evening Schools ...

Although support from public funds for denominational schools had been cut off after 1854, a close cooperation still existed in San Francisco. The Evening Schools of San Francisco had their beginnings through the cooperation of Archbishop Alemany with the Board of Education of San Francisco.

"During August, 1856, the Evening Schools were opened in the basement of the Cathedral, corner of California and Dupont Streets. They were first organized by Messrs. John Hamill, John Swett, Ahira Holmes, and James Denman, who volunteered their services until the Board of Education was convinced of the success of the schools and the importance and usefulness of the Evening School instruction. The Evening Schools have continued with varying success, until now they are among the most useful and prosperous of our Public Schools." (71)

The basement of the Cathedral continued to be used as a parish school until the fire and earthquake of 1906. During the life of St. Mary's as the first Cathedral of San Francisco hundreds of the young men who were later to be leaders of San Francisco were educated within those familiar walls which were the heart of Catholicism in San Francisco.

St. Mary's Temperance, Benevolent and Library Association ...

With the news of the discovery of gold in California, January 24, 1848, thousands abandoned their former livelihood and undertook the dangerous journey by land or sea to the gold strike. For the many who saw only the gold fields as their goal, scarcely a handful hoped to take up their former occupations when they reached California. For a few mad years the pursuit of gold intoxicated the whole population. But when the fabulous years of the 1850's had yielded to the better organized 1860's, the people of California began to turn to social organizations. This trend was reflected in the building of the numerous halls and theatres of San Francisco.

Although the author has been unable to establish the beginnings of the St. Mary's Temperance, Benevolent and Library Association, this organization had achieved sufficient popularity to receive notice in the public press by 1867. On January 26, 1867, *The Monitor* reported:

St. Mary's Temperance Benevolent and Library Association

There was a large and enthusiastic meeting of the above named association in the basement of the Cathedral on Thursday evening last. Over two hundred members were present, and the pledge was administered by the Chaplain, Rev. Father Harrington, to a large number of new members.

As indicated in the above quotation, the clergy of St. Mary's Cathedral were actively interested in sponsoring this organization. Not only were the Cathedral clergy interested in assisting the members to practice temperance, but they were also zealous in securing for them the benefits which an appealing benevolent and literary association could bring to the members. The Rev. Father Harrington of St. Mary's Cathedral, who was chaplain of the association, addressed the meeting referred to above, and announced that Archbishop Alemany, to assist the association in its work, was desirous of presenting the members with the library of St. Mary's Cathedral, and of presenting facilities at the Cathedral where this library might be enjoyed by the members. (72)

As a means of assisting the association to build a reserve in its treasury, the Rev. James Chrysostom Bouchard, S. J. (cf. p. 39) offered to give a benefit lecture at the Cathedral. On February 2, 1867, the Catholic newspaper, *The Monitor,* carried a notice of this coming lecture together with a statement of the literary and benevolent aims of the association. This notice reads:

FATHER BOUCHARD'S LECTURE

We noticed briefly, last week, that Father Buchard (Sic) will deliver a lecture at St. Mary's Cathedral, in this city, on Thursday evening, February 7, for the benefit of St. Mary's Temperance, Benevolent Library Association. The subject of the Rev. Lecturer will be, "The Catholic Church, the Source of Security in Life and Death." The proceeds of the lecture will be used for the establishment of a Catholic Library and Reading Room. The price of admission will be only fifty cents . . . The Association is destined to be one of great usefulness. In addition to its influence in the cause of temperance and benevolence, it will furnish the means for profitable and pleasurable mental employment to its members in the library and reading room. We are informed that the Most Rev. Alemany has donated to it a library and that he also designs fitting up a hall for its use, which

33

will be erected as soon as the weather will permit. The librarian will keep a register of the names of all the members out of employment, so that they may receive the assistance of other members in obtaining it and also for the purpose of affording those who wish to engage the services of others interested an opportunity to secure those who are known to be good, sober, industrious persons. Thus, it will be seen, that the Association will accomplish good in various ways. It is gratifying to know that its roll of membership is already a long one, and we trust that ere long it will embrace thousands of names.

This assistance to the Association by Father Bouchard was two-fold in that it not only attracted to the Cathedral a large audience who would be acquainted with the purposes of the Association, but also realized a considerable sum for the treasury. *The Monitor,* (San Francisco), for February 9, 1867, reports the complete success of this lecture:

FATHER BOUCHARD'S LECTURE

The audience which assembled last Thursday evening at St. Mary's Cathedral to hear the lecture of Rev. Father Bouchard on "The Catholic Church, the Source of Security in Life and Death," was a very large and attentive one. The lecture itself was an exceedingly interesting one, and was abundant in eloquence, logic, and research. It was delivered in that happy and impressive style for which Father Bouchard is so eminently celebrated.

On Thursday evening, February 14, 1867, at 7 P.M., the library and reading room of St. Mary's Temperance and Benevolent Society was opened. A meeting was held in the basement of St. Mary's Cathedral to mark the occasion to which the public was invited. It was announced at this meeting that the library and reading room would be opened to the general public who could enjoy its privileges by paying a one dollar initiation fee and one dollar per quarter for the use of the library. It was further pointed out that it is not necessary for those who wish to avail themselves of the library to become members of the Temperance and Benevolent Association. (73)

On January 8, 1868, after the regular business of the Temperance and Benevolent Society had been completed and eighty new members had come forward to take the pledge of temperance, the meeting, which was held in the basement of the Cathedral, was addressed by Archbishop Alemany. He gave an impressive and eloquent

34

discourse on the value of the Association and invited many of the non-members who attended to join the organization. (74)

Although many of the more prominent Catholics had moved from the Cathedral Parish to the newer districts of San Fransisco because of the unwholesome surroundings and evil social conditions which were beginning to appear in the vicinity of the Cathedral, nevertheless, the St. Mary's Temperance Benevolent and Library Association continued to enjoy great popularity with the Catholics of the city. Because of the increased membership and interest in the organization, in January of 1870, the constitution of the organization was revised and members would receive, in case of illness, seven dollars per week besides the services of an eminent physician free and on the death of a member, his family would receive from the Association between four and five hundred dollars. (75)

As the strength and popularity of this Association increased through the years, it was decided at a regular meeting held on May 3, 1873, that Woodward's Gardens, a popular recreation area of San Francisco (76) would be the scene of the annual picnic of the Association.

By means of funds derived from this annual picnic, the St. Mary's Temperance Benevolent and Library Association achieved its aims by providing needed help to its members who formed a substantial portion of the Catholic population of San Francisco. It provided for these members, through its library and the services of prominent men who lectured at its meeings in the basement of St. Mary's Cathedral, a knowledge of current issues and an opportunity for education in cultural and Catholic matters. It provided wholesome recreation which materially assisted its members in observing the temperance pledge. Finally, it provided financial assistance for those members who could not obtain assistance from other agencies in San Francisco at this time.

Thus it can readily be seen St. Mary's Cathedral furnished through these organizations an important contribution to the cultural, educational, and social needs of this growing city at a time when such a contribution was most necessary. It served to balance off the tremendous strides in financial and economic development the city was undergoing.

Old St. Mary's Church
Interior
After 1927 Enlargement

PART THREE

GREAT DAYS IN THE LIFE OF ST. MARY'S CATHEDRAL

The holocaust of earthquake and fire which tumbled in the roof and melted down the stained glass windows of Old St. Mary's on April 18, 1906, could not completely purge out of the brick walls some part of the emotion which swelled up from the throngs that crowded it on great days during its life as a Cathedral. As the heart of Catholic life in San Francisco, it was only fitting that this structure should serve as a stage upon which these events, great in the drama of that same life, should be enacted. Since any sketch of the history of St. Mary's Cathedral, brief though it may be, would be incomplete without some mention of the great events which transpired within the walls during its lifetime, the author intends to treat some of the more important of these great days.

Archbishop Alemany Receives the Pallium . . .

On the 18th of November, 1855, the Right Reverend Thaddeus Amat (1811-1878), first Bishop of Monterey and Los Angeles, as a personal representative of Pope Pius IX, conferred upon Archbishop Alemany the Pallium as first Metropolitan of the Archdiocese of San Francisco. The large area of the Cathedral, the galleries, and even the vestibules were crowded to inconvenience with a most respectful congregation. The ceremonies of the conferring of the Pallium were preceded by a Pontifical Mass which was celebrated by Bishop Amat who preached a sermon very eloquent and suitable for the occasion. The choir, which was considerably increased, rendered in an excellent style and with great effect the music of the Mass composed for the occasion by Mr. George Loder. For many of those who were present the conferring of the Pallium was a new experience in matters Catholic.

This simple decoration worn around the neck having a humeral and pectoral pendant and crosses extending to the shoulders on either side is the insignia of a Metropolitan in his Archdiocese. Now, for the first time they were aware of the organization of the Catholic Church in California. A Church which had grown in a few short

Reverend Claude J. Collins C.S.P.
Present Pastor
Old St. Mary's Church

years from an orphaned diocese without a bishop to a Province of the Catholic Church in North America guided by an Archbishop, Joseph Sadoc Alemany. (77)

Archbishop Alemany's Silver Jubilee . . .

Although Archbishop Alemany remained to the very end the humble Dominican Friar, nevertheless, in 1862, on the occasion of the twenty-fifth anniversary of his ordination to the priesthood, the clergy and the laity of the Archdiocese would not let the occasion pass without proper commemorative services. In all the churches of the Archdiocese, Mass was offered for the spiritual welfare of the Archbishop. Although it must have been contrary to the desire of Archbishop Alemany, who in his humility would have preferred to let the occasion pass without public observance of his Silver Jubilee, nevertheless, he yielded to the wishes of his clergy and celebrated Pontifical Mass for the occasion. As a tribute to the Archbishop on the occasion of his Silver Jubilee, his Vicar General, Very Reverend J. Prendergast (1834-1914), Right Reverend Bishop Amat, C.M., of Monterey and Los Angeles, Right Reverend Bishop O'Connell (78) of the Vicariate Apostolic of Marysville, and Reverend Francis Mora, (79) future Coadjutor Bishop of Monterey and Los Angeles were present, as well as many of the secular and regular clergy of the Province. In a sermon preached by Bishop Amat a very fitting tribute was paid to the work of Archbishop Alemany and the progress of the Church in California. The Cathedral was crowded with friends who wished to express by their presence the high regard in which they held their Archbishop. At one o'clock in the basement of the Cathedral a banquet was given by the clergy and they expressed their filial regard for Archbishop Alemany by presenting him with a magnificent set of gold vestments valued at $1,500. (80)

Archbishop Alemany Mourns a Friend — The Death of Pope Pius IX . . .

In 1878 when the news of the death of the Supreme Pontiff Pope Pius IX reached California, Archbishop Alemany immediately issued a Pastoral Letter in which he ordered that Masses be said throughout the diocese. (81) Also it was announced that on February 12, 1878, at 9:30 A.M., a Pontifical Mass of Requiem would be celebrated at the Cathedral for the late Sovereign Pontiff to which all who could attend, especially the clergy, were invited. In consequence of the announcement contained in the Pastoral Letter of Archbishop Alemany, St. Mary's Cathedral became the chief center of the solemn commemoration in the Catholic Community. The account of the ceremonies at the Cathedral were described in the press of the day as follows:

We may say that this was the first time that San Francisco was the scene of such solemn and imposing obsequies; for in 1846, when the deceased Pontiff was elected, there was not even the semblance of a city here. The Cathedral was, therefore, especially prepared for the ceremonies of Tuesday. The main entrance and the two side doors were draped with mourning emblems, as was also the entrance to the adjoining presbytery. On entering the sacred edifice a most impressive sight met the view. The long rows of pillars on each side were almost entirely concealed by drapery of white and black cloth. Only a subdued light was permitted to come through the windows, which were trimmed with similar drapery. Festoons of black cloth decked with white rosettes hung between the pillars, along the edge of the galleries and in front of the pews. The main altar had been denuded of its chief ornaments and nothing remained except the six great candlesticks which were covered with black. The sacred tabernacle was also appropriately decorated. In front of the altar and outside the communion rails was the catafalque. It was covered by a pall of black velvet, relieved with narrow bands of white, and trimmed with heavy silver fringe. On and surrounding the catafalque were floral tributes of rare beauty and exquisite design. On top were several large caskets of magnificent flowers, and at the end, facing the congregation was a design, in flowers also, representing the Papal arms, with tiara and crossed keys, with the name "Pio Nono" tastefully wrought in small white flowers, which was much admired. This, we understand, was the gift of D. J. Oliver, Esq. Six large candlesticks bearing wax candles were also placed on top amid the flowers; and beneath, attached to the catafalque, were the following inscriptions printed (remainder not legible).

In fact, every point of vantage that could be seized upon to decorate the interior of the Cathedral was availed of by skillful hands, and turned to the best possible account.

In consequence of the length of the prescribed ceremonies, the early hour of half past nine o'clock was determined upon as the time for them to be commenced. Long before that hour, however, early in the morning in fact, immense crowds wended their way to the Cathedral. Soon the

38

whole of the sacred edifice was closely thronged in every part, and those who came any way late had great difficulty in obtaining entrance at all. Thousands were, as might readily be imagined, unable to approach even the doors, and the congregation, so to speak, flowed out upon the sidewalk and into the middle of the street. This is the most striking proof we have ever seen of the utter inadequacy of St. Mary's to serve as a Cathedral Church to such a city as San Francisco much longer.

Precisely at the hour fixed, His Grace the Archbishop issued from the sanctuary and the solemn office for the dead, over which he presided, was immediately begun. Inside the railings was a large body of clergymen, among whom we noticed the following: (here are enumerated by name fifty-three priests among whom were Jesuits and Dominicans). Several of the Christian brothers were also present. His Grace, the Archbishop presided, and the chanters were Rev. Father Dempsey and Rev. Father McSweeney. The Catholics of this city are not unacquainted with the character of the ceremony, and it is therefore not necessary to describe it further than to say that it was far more than unusually impressive and that the singing was excellent.

After the conclusion of the Office for the Dead, the Pontifical Requiem Mass was begun. His Grace, the Archbishop was the celebrant; Rev. Father Harrington, assistant priest, Rev. Father McSweeney, deacon, Rev. Father Casey, sub-deacon, and Rev. Father Bowman, master of ceremonies. The music was that of Mozart's celebrated Requiem, with full choir and orchestra. The choir had been especially augmented for the occasion, and was effective in the highest degree. The instrumentation, too, was very fine. Taken altogether, the music was probably the most grand and solemn as well as the most purely ecclesiastical in character, ever heard inside a church edifice in this city. Professor William Toepke conducted. At the conclusion of the Mass the Archbishop ascended the pulpit and spoke as follows: (here follows a lengthy eulogy on Pius Ninth of which we quote the following).

"His pontifical hands, which had consecrated so many Priests and had confirmed (Sic) so many Bishops, and created so many Sees, and which had especially created this our Archiepiscopal See and Ecclesiastical Province of San Francisco, whose pontifical hands, which, for thirty-two years had been raised to bless the entire world, raised also to forgive his enemies, raised up daily to Heaven, even to his last breath, to invoke Christ's Holy Blessings on his universal flock, those kind hands with which he presented me that beautiful

39

chalice with which we have just celebrated for him the holy sacrifice, . . . those hands are now lowered and folded in death."

His Grace spoke very clearly and distinctly, so as to be heard by everyone in the immense audience. Yet it was evident that his Grace was deeply moved by the most sad occasion. The sermon was followed by the customary absolutions. These are five in number—one delivered by each of four priests, in the absence of as many prelates, standing at the corners of the catafalque, and the last by the Archbishop. The clergymen who performed this duty were Rev. Fathers Prendergast, Harrington, Grey and Dempsey. The absolution pronounced by his Grace brought the ceremonies to a conclusion. The vast congregation then dispersed, but so closely packed was the crowd that it was upwards of an hour before the passageways were even comparatively clear. (82)

Consecration of Bishop Manogue . . .

When Bishop Alemany received the news that he had been elevated to the rank of Archbishop and that the Pallium would soon be sent from Rome, he humorously remarked that he had completed his career—there remained only for him to die. (83) But there were many more great events in his life. Among the most significant days of his San Francisco episcopate was certainly the day on which he consecrated a priest who was especially dear to his heart, Father Patrick Manogue (1831-1895) as Coadjutor Bishop of Grass Valley. Young Patrick Manogue had come to California to seek his fortune as a gold miner at Moore's Flat, in present day Nevada County, when there was but one diocese for the entire western slope of the United States from Oregon to Mexico, for such was the Diocese of Monterey in 1852.

The Cathedral of St. Mary's was thronged with a large assemblage which completely filled the church on Sunday morning, January 16, 1881. It might well be imagined that among those who attended that day, there were some that whispered to their neighbor, "Patrick Manogue, I knew him as a miner at Moore's Flat. It's a fine Bishop we'll be getting for he is a man to be proud of." This well may have been said, for Patrick Manogue was a splendid specimen of manhood. He was more than six feet tall, in excellent physical health, in his fiftieth year of life, and reflecting in his person the active life among the mining communities of Nevada to which he ministered. (84)

40

The account of his consecration is taken from the *Daily Alta California* (San Francisco). This paper, which usually treated local items with brevity, on this occasion described the event in full detail:

A large assemblage completely filled the auditory of St. Mary's Cathedral yesterday morning to witness the imposing ceremonies connected with the consecration of Father P. Manogue, the new Bishop of the Nevada diocese (Sic) of the Catholic Church. The high altar and the side altars were beautifully decorated with rare flowers, whose fragrance mingled with the incense, while every decoration and the bright vestments of the officiating clergy shone brightly under the rays of the altar lights. The Most Reverend Archbishop Alemany acted as the celebrant, and was assisted by Rt. Rev. E. O'Connell, Bishop of Grass Valley, and Right Reverend Francis Mora, Bishop of Monterey and Los Angeles. Very Reverend J. Prendergast, Vicar General of the Diocese (Sic), officiated as assistant priest, while Very Reverend Thomas Dalton, Vicar General of Grass Valley and Very Reverend Father Richardson of Los Angeles, acted as Deacons of Honor. The Deacons and sub-Deacons of the Mass were Rev. Hugh Logan and Rev. P. J. Cummins. Rev. Father Harrington, of St. Francis Church, acted as Master of Ceremonies at the Pontifical Mass, and Rev. George Montgomery, assisted by Rev. Father John Sullivan officiated as Master of Ceremonies at the Consecration. (85)

One wonders what thoughts passed through the Archbishop's mind when Father Manogue presented himself before the Archbishop for consecration. Did he live again those early days when he was a new Archbishop in a new and struggling Archdiocese? Did he remember accepting the young Irish miner, Patrick Manogue, as a candidate to the priesthood and sending him to St. Sulpice to study? If his mind did not revert to those early days, it must have done so when Father James Bouchard ascended the pulpit and introduced his sermon with the text:

"And you also shall bear witness,
Because you have been with me from the beginning."
St. John XV,27.

The Archbishop Departs . . .

Wednesday, May 27, 1885, marked the end of an era in the ecclesiastical history of San Francisco, for on that day Archbishop Joseph Sadoc Alemany, the first Archbishop of San Francisco, left his Archdiocese never to return. It was probably the saddest day of his life. Not as a father but more as a mother he had taken the infant

41

diocese of Monterey, which later became the Archdiocese of San Francisco (1853) under his protection and through his loving, watchful care had watched it grow into the well organized, well established, prosperous Archdiocese which he had resigned to his successor, Archbishop Patrick Riordan.

On Saturday, May 23, prior to his departure, he spent the evening in the confessional. Literally hundreds of San Franciscans from all walks of life, whom he had guided in matters of religion for years, approached their beloved Archbishop and heard from him in the quiet moment of the confessional, the parting words of spiritual guidance and received absolution for the last time from the devoted shepherd of their souls. For years it had been the practice of the Archbishop to sit in this same confessional in order that his children might have free access to the spiritual guidance of their Archbishop.

At 7:30 o'clock Sunday morning, May 24, he stood at the altar of St. Mary's Cathedral in the presence of a congregation which packed every seat, aisle, and nook of the edifice. He celebrated Mass and then for the last time in the Cathedral which he had caused to be built, distributed Holy Communion. He was unassisted in this task preferring to do this last office with his own hand, bestowing his benediction on the kneeling communicants. It seemed that everyone in the Cathedral pressed forward to receive their last communion from the Archbishop and the Mass was delayed because of their numbers.

After a short rest he again entered the Cathedral and assisted at the celebration of a Pontifical Mass by Archbishop Riordan. As the choir finished Mozart's Twelfth Mass the aged Archbishop rose and walked to the center of the altar and began a confirmation address to several hundred children who were gathered about the altar to receive the sacrament. The girls were dressed in white with wreaths of flowers on their heads and the boys were dressed in black suits. They knelt quietly at the altar while the Archbishop spoke to them. He was deeply moved by the scene. His eyes filled with tears and his voice quavered with emotion. Through his mind must have passed the memory of that first Christmas Day, thirty-one years before, when he, as the first Archbishop, sang the first Pontifical Mass in this same Cathedral.

As he proceeded with his discourse he became very earnest and

42

although the children kneeling before him were not forgotten, his thoughts turned to his co-laborers on the altar beside him and the old familiar faces in the congregation. His sermon turned to a topic which was familiar to his listeners, "The Immortality of the Soul." The deep spirituality of Archbishop Alemany in this moment of great emotion poured forth on his lips in the form of a humble appeal to his co-workers to carry on the great work which is the mission of the Church, "The Salvation of Souls."

As the Archbishop concluded his eloquent address he was overcome with emotion. Tears were in the eyes of those with him on the altar and the congregation was moved to tears by the words which seemed to them as though they had fallen from the lips of a prophet of old. At the conclusion of the confirmation ceremony, and with a final blessing imparted by the Prelate, the congregation slowly filed out of the Cathedral with the feeling in their hearts that one destined to be accounted great in the life of Catholicism in California would soon pass out of their lives. Although he was still an active man, in spite of his seventy-one years, Archbishop Alemany's steps were slow as he passed out of the Cathedral for the last time. Although we know from Archbishop Alemany's life and actions that he laid down his heavy burden of the Episcopacy without regret, nevertheless, as he looked back upon his Cathedral which he had watched grow from Chinese stone, New England brick, and California redwoods, in those early years, 1853-1854, he must have felt the pain of parting with an old friend with whom he had spent many a peaceful hour in the turmoil of his busy labors. (86)

Cardinal Gibbons at St. Mary's Cathedral . . .

On Sunday, October 23, 1887, His Eminence Cardinal Gibbons (1834-1921) (87) presided at solemn service held at. St. Mary's Cathedral at 10:30 A.M. His visit to California had attracted widespread notice and the announcement that he would preach at the services had drawn a large number of people to the Cathedral. The crowd was so large that many were forced to remain outside and they remained standing in the vicinity of the Cathedral waiting for the sight of his Eminence as he would depart after the services. The Cathedral, itself, was ablaze with candles, the side altar and main altar were decorated with flowers and the entire interior was festooned with evergreens and ornamented throughout with numerous floral devices. The High Mass was sung by the Reverend D. D.

Chapelle. The music for the Mass was furnished by members of St. Mary's choir under the direction of Professor Eimer.

At the first gospel his Eminence Cardinal Gibbons, who had occupied the Archiepiscopal throne during the ceremonies, arose, ascended the pulpit and spoke at length to the Catholics of California who crowded the Cathedral. At the conclusion of the ceremonies Cardinal Gibbons left the church and rested for a brief time at the Episcopal residence. He then proceeded to the steps of St. Mary's Cathedral and permitted the faithful to approach and kiss the amethyst finger ring which he wore. It was necessary to interrupt the number of people who pressed forward to kiss the Cardinal's ring in order that he might review the parade of the Young Men's Institute which was passing before the Cathedral and marching in his honor. At the conclusion of this demonstration he bestowed his benediction upon the immense concourse of people which now thronged all the streets approaching the Cathedral. (88)

PART FOUR

THE NEED FOR A NEW CATHEDRAL

The Need for a New Cathedral ...

When Benjamin E. Lloyd, in 1876, published his descriptive work of San Francisco, *Lights and Shades in San Francisco,* he reflected the attitude of Archbishop Alemany, himself, and most of the Catholics when he described the surroundings of St. Mary's Cathedral as follows:

On the corner of California and Stockton Streets stands Grace Church; but a block below, at the corner of California and Dupont Streets, is St. Mary's Cathedral. In one, the wealthiest and most aristocratic Episcopal congregation in the city worships, in the other, the pride of Catholicism in San Francisco praises God for His Blessings. Devout Christians assemble at these churches and engage in the solemn service of sanctuary. The loveliest of lovely women and noble men thither repair upon the Sabbath Day, and unite their voices in praise and thanksgiving for the goodness and mercy of the Lord that has continually followed them. Within those walls there is evidence that this is a Christian City— a block away the streets are lined with houses of prostitution; and a stone's throw beyond is the Barbary Coast reeking in infamous filth.

Nearly half a score of churches point their spires heavenward in this immediate vicinity indicating the upward way that leads to life; two days in every week the bells in those steeples sound the call to assemble and worship, and the worshipers who meet in these temples of religion accept the Bible that pronounces a great woe upon the workers of iniquity; that visits vengeance upon crime; that utters a curse upon adultery; that denounces harlotry as one of the most dangerous evils, and sets up the warning, "Beware! go not in her way!" ...

Dupont Street, running parallel to this scene, is likewise in its gayest dress. But how different is the picture! There are upon the street sulking groups of men with muffled faces, who seek its darkest side lest they be recognized by others likewise shunning observation; bold, boisterous fellows, uttering oaths and obscene jests; but not a single female form is seen unless it be a flittering figure moving rapidly along and suddenly *disappearing in another street. But peeping through the window shutters, or standing at the thresholds, door after door, block after block are wo-men whose calling is branded on their foreheads, may be recognized in the twinkling of their eyes, and is boldly called out to you as you pass along the walk. The doors are left slightly ajar, or the blinds turned, so that he who will may look within. In their rooms is a warm, hazy light and everything is invitingly arranged. Almost every passer-by is hailed and invited in. If he declines, he is urged; and if he still refuses, he is entreated and sometimes taken by the hand and playfully forced to enter. These are some of San Francisco's inconsistencies. It is a disgrace to San Fran-cisco, a stain upon her brow; but it is more disgraceful to those property holders and speculators who permit their tenement houses to be used for such vile purposes. (89)*

Archbishop Alemany Proposes a New Cathedral . . .

Archbishop Alemany was well aware of the sordid conditions existing within the shadow of the Cathedral. It is probable that the low element in this neighborhood offered occasional insult to the Archbishop. The life and actions of this Prelate must have shamed even the most hardened of the wretched inhabitants of this irrelig-ious, immoral neighborhood. In their embarrassment they probably sought to ease their discomfort by committing unwarranted affronts to his person and calling. However, he was perfectly willing to sub-mit to these occasional affronts provided it was not detrimental to the cause of religion. He had vigorously sought to eliminate the vice and sordidness which had grown up in this area, but the persons responsible for permitting these conditions to exist did not yet prefer decency to graft and corruption. Nor was he embarrassed to receive distinguished visitors in these shabby surroundings.

Cardinal Vaughan (cf. supra) when he visited California in 1864 described the residence where Archbishop Alemany had lived for the first ten years of his archiepiscopal rule:

"Go, then up California Street in San Francisco, turn around the Cathedral of St. Mary's, and you will enter a miserable, dingy little house. This is the residence of the Archbishop of San Francisco. . . . To the left are a number of little yards, and the back windows of houses in which Chinamen are swarming. Broken pots, and pans, old doors, sides of pig glazed and varnished, long strings of meat (God only knows what meat!) hanging to dry, dog kennels, dead cats, dirty linen in heaps, such is the view on the left. The odors which exhale from it who shall describe?

To the right, adjoining the Cathedral, is a yard where stands a little iron or zinc cottage, containing two rooms; this is where the Archbishop lives. One is his bedroom, and the other is his office, where his secretaries are at work all day. No man is more poorly lodged in the whole city, and no man better preaches the spirit of evangelical poverty and detachment in the midst of this money-worshipping city than this Dominican Spanish Archbishop of San Francisco." (90)

Archbishop Alemany Purchases A Site . . .

Two years before Archbishop Riordan came to California, (1883) to assist Archbishop Alemany as coadjutor, the need for a new Cathedral became so pressing that Archbishop Alemany undertook the preliminary steps to secure it. In August of 1881, Archbishop Alemany issued a pastoral letter in which he pointed out "the necessity of removing the Cathedral from its objectionable location to some more respectable and suitable part of the city." (91)

However, the response of the Catholics to Alemany's appeal for a new Cathedral was not as great as expected. On August 26, 1881, he appointed the Reverend John McGinty (1855-1918) to the exclusive work of encouraging and collecting donations with which to secure a site for the Cathedral. The Archbishop clearly pointed out that it was not for his own personal satisfaction that he wished a new Cathedral, but that rather for the love of God and for the love of religion a suitable new Cathedral was necessary for the Archdiocese.

On March 22, 1882, the editor of *The Monitor*, (San Francisco), was proud to announce:

At length we are in a position to congratulate the Catholics of California upon the completion of the preliminary plans for the erection of the long contemplated and much needed new St. Mary's Cathedral. The site chosen is one of the most healthy portions of the city and is sufficiently elevated to make the contemplated cathedral an object to be seen from different points. Instead of being—as is the case of the present edifice— in the midst of a neighborhood inhabited by persons of the lowest character, the new cathedral will be surrounded by the mansions of many of the most respectable citizens, and hence the very disagreeable necessity of changing the site of a cathedral will be avoided in the future. (92)

During he next year, Archbishop Alemany was busily engaged in collecting the money with which to pay for the site selected on

Van Ness and O'Farrell Streets. When Archbishop Patrick Riordan was consecrated in Chicago as Coadjutor Archbishop of San Francisco on September 16, 1883, Archbishop Alemany delayed the plans for building the new Cathedral until the arrival of his Coadjutor. At this time, however, the fate of St. Mary's Cathedral was undecided. Two possibilities presented themselves to Archbishop Alemany; he could either raze the present Cathedral and use the material in the erection of a smaller church in some suitable locality east of Powell Street, for the convenience of those Catholics who were adjacent thereto, or he could leave the building intact as a parish church. (93)

Archbishop Riordan Proposes To Build ...

Because Archbishop Alemany was resigning and was shifting the heavy burden of the affairs of the Archdiocese to the shoulders of his young Coadjutor, Archbishop Riordan, no further action on the building of the Cathedral was taken until after Archbishop Alemany's departure (May 27, 1885). In December of 1885, Archbishop Riordan addressed the following words to the Catholics of his Archdiocese:

The location of the present Cathedral is such that it can scarcely be approached from any direction without a shudder at the sinfulness and filth of its surroundings, hence—even for no other reason the necessity of a new Cathedral in a more secluded and respectable location, is one of the greatest and most pressing wants of this Archdiocese. (94)

In order to encourage the Catholics of the Archdiocese to vigorously support this program for the building of a new Cathedral, he contrasted the situation when Archbishop Alemany built his Cathedral with the present condition of Catholicism in California. He referred to those days as follows:

The present Cathedral was built in 1852-1853, at a time when there were scarcely Catholics enough in all California to fill it, yet such was the liberal spirit manifested by the generous Catholic pioneers that they accomplished a work then which was the wonder and admiration of all people on the Pacific Coast. (95)

Because of the sordid surroundings about St. Mary's Cathedral, Archbishop Riordan removed his residence to St. John Baptist Church (96) on Eddy Street between Octavia and Laguna Streets. This remained his residence until the dedication of the new Van Ness Avenue Cathedral, January 11, 1891, when St. John the Baptist

48

parish was suppressed and the area became the new Cathedral parish.

On May 5, 1886, *The Monitor* (San Francisco) gave the following account of Archbishop Riordan's report on the progress of the building of the new Cathedral:

At the conclusion of last Mass in St. John's Church, Eddy Street, on last Sunday morning, Archbishop Riordan took for his topic the subject of Cathedrals, and in alluding to the contemplated new Cathedral for this Archdiocese his Grace stated that at least $200,000 would be required to erect the building exclusive of the final decorations. Of this amount $100,000 has been promised by the wealthy Catholics of this city and $60,000 thereof has been already paid in. For the other $100,000 he looks to the poorer in worldly wealth among the members of his flock. Father Prendergast, the Archbishop stated, had already commenced the collection of contributions and a commitee would be appointed to receive donations from $500 down. This sum could be paid in three installments—the first during this year and the others during the two following years. The work will not be confined to those in the present and future Cathedral Parishes, but will be extended to others throughout the Archdiocese. All those desirous of giving over $500 are requested to call upon the Archbishop.

The lot upon which the Cathedral will be built was paid for before the departure of Archbishop Alemany, but the work of grading it will require an expenditure of about $12,000. The Archbishop confidently hopes to be able to lay the cornerstone by the latter part of June or the 1st of July, and the work will then be continued steadily and as rapidly as the funds will permit and the probabilities are that the basement portion of the new edifice will be completed within the present year, and by the end of 1887, the walls and entire superstructure will be completed. The following year will be devoted to finishing the interior. (97)

The work was advanced rapidly and, according to schedule, the cornerstone of San Francisco's second Catholic Cathedral was laid May 1, 1890, and the Cathedral dedicated on Sunday, January 11, 1891.

Although Archbishop Riordan had officiated on special occasions at St. Mary's on California Street and Dupont during the period of his residence at St. John's, he did so because St. John's Church was a small frame building unsuitable for these occasions. Nevertheless, Old St. Mary's, as it now came to be known did not cease to be the Cathedral until Archbishop Riordan dedicated his new Cathedral, January 11, 1891, which was the solemn and final close of a great chapter in the story of San Francisco Catholicism for on that date the Catholics of the Archdiocese of San Francisco witnessed the dedication of their magnificent new Cathedral on Van Ness Avenue and O'Farrell Streets.

Conclusion . . .

On January 5, 1891, the San Francisco *Examiner* carried the following notice:

St. Mary's Cathedral on California and Dupont Streets was practically closed yesterday at the celebration of the last High Mass held in the church.

In the future the edifice will be known as St. Mary's Church. It will be from this time forth simply a place of worship for the convenience of those who are so domiciled as to be unable to attend any other church or the new Cathedral.

The disorderly element which had crowded in about St. Mary's Cathedral on California and Dupont Streets made a new location for the Cathedral imperative. The Archbishop of San Francisco could not pontificate within a stone's throw of the lowest dregs of corruption. The new Cathedral on Van Ness Avenue and O'Farrell Street would be dedicated on the following Sunday, January 11, 1891, and it was believed at that time that St. Mary's Church, as it was now called, on California and Dupont Streets, would be used temporarily until the Catholic population of that neighborhood could be served by some other parish church, and then closed.

But the church that played so great a part in the story of early San Francisco Catholicism was not to face such an end. Three years later, in 1894, the church was entrusted to the Fathers of the Congregation of St. Paul, familiarly referred to as Paulist Fathers. Since that time Old St. Mary's, as it is affectionately called, and which name the passage of time has sanctioned, has been in the charge of the Paulist Fathers.

The earthquake and fire on Wednesday, April 18, 1906, gutted the interior of the building but the massive brick walls and tower still stood. When the architects found, upon examination, that the walls were virtually unharmed by both the earthquake and fire, it was decided to rebuild Old St. Mary's. Although plans were made to close the old Cathedral in 1891, they were not carried out, and although gutted in the earthquake and fire of 1906, Old St. Mary's was yet to add further chapters to the story of Catholicism in San Francisco. In 1929 the building was enlarged and the interior completely remodeled.

The great number of worshippers who throng Old St. Mary's each day of the week testify to the place that this building, which served so long and so well as San Francisco's First Cathedral, still has in the religious life of the city. Just as its erection represented an act of faith and confidence on Archbishop Alemany's part in the future of the city (an act of faith fully justified by subsequent events) so, too, the integral part now played by Old St. Mary's Church, in the community it serves, is a testimonial to the sagacity of Archbishop Alemany in building so permanently and so well. Old St. Mary's no longer is the Cathedral, but at the present time it is certainly one of the most distinguished Catholic Churches in the city.

In 1854, the city was largely built of tents and flimsy shacks. The casual visitor wrote home letters of the tent town of San Francisco and the immorality that was rampant. But with the erection of this Cathedral, standing high on the hill overlooking the long since vanished cove, the visitor, even before he stepped ashore, could realize the permanence to come. It also gave the citizens of San Francisco confidence in their own city. It established the center of the Archdiocese in San Francisco and weakened the pretensions of Benicia as the principal metropolis of the Bay Area. The Cathedral cross silhouetted on the city skyline was a silent but conclusive argument that morality and religion were practiced by those who were conscious of their obligations. In a word, St. Mary's Cathedral in 1854 made a permanent, organized, religious island in a welter of transient, orderless immorality. During its lifetime as a Cathedral it was the center of Catholic life. It drew Catholics within its walls to solve their present needs and give substance to their future aspirations. From its basement flowed the educational, cultural, and social development of Catholics and non-Catholics alike. It was not the only great church in San Francisco; but it was one of the few great churches in San Francisco when such churches were so badly needed. Old St. Mary's church is still carrying on the work, but in a special manner; while a Cathedral, St. Mary's for thirty-six years was synonymous with what was decent, wholesome, cultural, and uplifting in San Francisco.

51

St. Mary's Catholic Chinese Mission 1951

PART FIVE

OLD ST. MARY'S

SAN FRANCISCO'S PAULIST CHURCH

(1894 - 1951)

The Intervening Years ...

After the new Cathedral on Van Ness Avenue was opened for worship, Old St. Mary's declined in ecclesiastical importance in San Francisco. As previously stated, the former Cathedral had reverted to a simple parish church under the title of St. Mary the Virgin. Reverend John J. Sullivan (1857-1920) was appointed pastor but served only a short time (1891-1892). He was followed in 1892 by the Reverend Thomas Larkin (1843-1906) who continued as pastor until the Paulists were entrusted with the care of the parish in 1894.

It must not be believed that Old St. Mary's had fallen upon such evil days that the services were poorly attended. The inference is made, from time to time, that when the Paulist Fathers were given charge of the parish the church knew only the occasional tread of a handful of parishioners. In fact, on the occasion of the Paulists accepting the responsibility of the parish the secular press stated:

Of late years the old church has been neglected, only a few families clinging to the parish, little more than a memory of its former strength and magnificence. (98)

The truth can in no way detract from the magnificent work that has been accomplished at Old St. Mary's under the able and zealous efforts of the Paulists. But the true state of affairs at Old St. Mary's in 1894 reveals quite the opposite of an empty church. The great problem was not a handful of families but literally hundreds of transient Catholics needing spiritual ministration and guidance. We read in the official Catholic paper of the Archdiocese:

Large congregations attend each service at St. Mary's. Many people imagine that because the Church is not in the residence portion of the city there is a slim attendance at Mass. While St. Mary's is not in a home section, proper, still it is in the hotel center and each Sunday, there is a

St. Mary's Chapel
in
St. Mary's Catholic Chinese Mission

large attendance from this source. There is not a vacant seat in the church unless in the galleries. St. Mary's choir is one of the best in the city. The music of each service is of a high order. (99)

The problem of Old St. Mary's was not to fill its empty pews because the Church was well attended at Mass. Rather it was the problem of ministering to the spiritual needs of the hundreds of transient Catholics, widely differing in background, who came to services at Old St. Mary's. It was not a parish of families but of businessmen and travelers. Here was a problem that needed very special treatment to be effectively solved. Archbishop Riordan wisely saw the solution in the work of the Paulists of whom he had recent first-hand knowledge.

The Coming of the Paulist Fathers ...

To the casual observer there is little connection between Old St. Mary's Church and the Paulists. It is merely a parish Church — one of half a hundred — through which the Paulists carry on their great work. But actually ties of origin and growth bind together this revered old Church and this energetic young religious congregation. We say "old Church" for these walls have stood for almost a century. We say "young congregation" for the American Congregation of St. Paul the Apostle was begun less than a hundred years ago which makes it young compared to the older religious orders which have existed for many centuries.

The close association between Old St. Mary's and the Paulist Fathers can be seen in the coincidence of dates. In 1852 Father Isaac Thomas Hecker (1819-1888) (100) began his missionary work as a Redemptorist. In this same year, Bishop (later Archbishop) Alemany was formulating plans for the building of his new Cathedral. In 1888 Father Hecker, by now the founder of the Paulist Fathers, and Archbishop Alemany, the builder of Old St. Mary's died. In 1894 a new and vigorous life was given to Old St. Mary's and the work of the Paulists when, after centering their work in New York City, the first branch of the Paulist Fathers was established at Old St. Mary's.

Paulist missionaries had been conducting missions in San Francisco and throughout the Far West since the 1870's. (101) Under the leadership of Father George Deshon (1823-1903), one of the founders of the community, they preached and labored in this Western country and left a great tradition of missionary ac-

53

tivity. Through the years the Paulist community continued to send missionaries to the Far West to conduct missions and help fill the pressing need for priests in outlying communities.

On January 20, 1894, at the invitation of Archbishop Riordan, two Paulist missionaries, Father Edward Bernard Brady (1847-1895) and Henry Harrison Wyman (1849-1929) gave a mission at St. Peter's Church, San Francisco. Fathers Brady and Wyman continued to conduct missions in parishes of San Francisco and the Bay Area for the remainder of the year. During this year Father Brady continually urged the Superior General of the Paulists to accept a parish in San Francisco. Archbishop Riordan had offered Father Brady Old St. Mary's when the latter was visiting San Francisco in 1890. But it was not until 1894 that Father Brady could convince Father Deshon, who was administering the community because of Father Hewitt's (1820-1897) failing health, that the first branch of the Paulist Fathers should be established in San Francisco. (103) A tradition which cannot be confirmed recounts that when Archbishop Riordan offered Father Brady a parish Old St. Mary's was suggested. The Archbishop protested that it was too unrepresentative to serve as an initial branch house for the Paulists. Father Brady then selected, as the only other alternative, a parish located in the wealthiest section of the city. Archbishop Riordan caught the humor of Father Brady's selection and said that since he could not give up the other parish, which accounted for half the revenue of the diocese, he must offer Father Brady Old St. Mary's. The fact that Father Brady was trying to interest the Paulist Superior General in taking over Old St. Mary's may well have influenced Archbishop Riordan not to close the venerable edifice when it ceased to be the Cathedral in 1891.

In 1894, when the Paulists took over Old St. Mary's or St. Mary's the Virgin, as the former Cathedral was then called, the work of the Paulist Fathers was sufficiently well known, and Old St. Mary's so fond a landmark, to attract the following notice in the daily press:

Paulists Here Permanently
Archbishop Riordan Transfers Old
St. Mary's Cathedral to
The Missionaries
One of The Ancient Landmarks

54

Old St. Mary's Cathedral on California Street, once the seat of ecclesiastical authority of the Roman Catholic Church in all California, yesterday closed that chapter of its history which marks its parochial career. Now it is a missionary Church and with the residence adjoining will be the permanent headquarters of the Paulist Community of priests on the Pacific Coast.

The transfer was made known from the pulpit by Archbishop Riordan at vespers last evening. The Archbishop said that he had had in mind for years the thought of having the Paulists permanently located in this city. He touched briefly upon the history of the community, paying the missionaries high tribute for their zeal and devotion to the cause of humanity.

Father Brodey (sic) who will be superior of the San Francisco community, also preached during the evening. The Church was packed to the doors with people. (104)

As stated in this article, December 9, 1894, marked a turning point in the history of Old St. Mary's Church. St. Mary's fame as the Cathedral on California Street had passed in 1891, but a newer phase was soon to start.

Heroic Beginnings ...

Although we have said Old St. Mary's was crowded at Sunday services, the affairs of the parish were in difficult straits. Two major problems faced the Paulist Fathers. Both problems were closely connected and both had to be successfully solved before Old St. Mary's could become the radiating heart of Paulist missionary activities in the Far West. The first problem was to revitalize Old St. Mary's as a parish. The second was to eliminate the sordid surroundings which pushed the stench of corruption to the very doors of the Church.

The first problem of revitalizing Old St. Mary's as a parish was attacked with vigor. Father Brady's great contribution to the struggle was to convince his Paulist Superior that he should accept the parish. Called by death, in four brief months his struggle was over as, on April 13, 1895, he laid down the burden of first pastor of the revitalized Old St. Mary's. Upon Father Brady's death, his confrere in so many missions, Father Wyman, succeeded him as pastor.

55

In the first issue of "The Parish Record and Church Calendar of Old St. Mary's Church," August, 1897, the following societies were listed as functioning: The Altar Society, The Ladies Aid Society, The League of the Sacred Heart, The Reading Circle, The Sunday School, The Calvarian Society, The Catholic Truth Society, and for non-Catholics and adults, instruction classes twice a week. Material improvements to the church fabric were considerable during the first three years of Paulist control, and were listed by Father Wyman himself. He thus wrote in the Church Calendar:

The beginning of the New Year suggests the appropriateness of a little chat on parish affairs in general. St. Paul boasted of what he had accomplished and how hard he had labored for the welfare of his brethern. We may be pardoned for indulging in a few words in the same strain at this time.

What has been accomplished for the parish in the material order, is, indeed, a source of gratification. Three years ago the Church sidewalk consisted of old planks, which had done good service, but were neither beautiful to behold nor pleasant to tread upon. Today we have a sidewalk that ought to please the most fastidious.

The Church itself — architecturally so beautiful — demanded immediate attention within and without. Its renovation was begun interiorly by the application of three coats of paint, which dispelled the "murky gloom," and gave to the begrimed walls and ceiling a bright and cheerful aspect. It cannot be called elaborate frescoeing, but good critics have commended the general effect.

The windows were plain glass and not in keeping with the received ideas of what church windows ought to be. Mr. Frank J. Sullivan generously donated one of the large stained glass windows in the sanctuary. The other was given by the Hon. James D. Phelan. Their example was speedily followed by ten others whose names we shall not mention here, as several wished to remain unknown. All the windows on both sides of the nave, with the exception of two, have already been given, and we expect these remaining two to be placed in position by Easter, as several have intimated their intention of giving a memorial window.

Angels have taken their stand above the sanctuary with raised trumpets to sound a warning of the judgment. The dim gaslight has given place to its formidable rival — electricity — which has expelled all the shadows of the galleries.

The exterior of the Church has received the much needed aid of artisans. The crumbling stone trimmings, which were a menace to life, *have been cut away and replaced by substantial material. The painters have covered the walls with several red coats which ought to protect them from the ravages of the weather for some time to come. The old tower clock has been coaxed from its erratic movements and once again announces in clear tones, and with accuracy, the fleeting hours. The parochial residence has likewise been renovated and made a pleasant dwelling place. (105)*

But it must not be assumed the Paulist Fathers were concentrating their activities solely to Old St. Mary's parish. Not only were the Paulists continuing their parochial missions throughout Northern California but they devoted considerable time to social services of the city. It was the newly formed Paulist parish which undertook the care of transient sailors who visited this great port city. On January 1, 1898, at number 9 Mission Street, near the heart of the waterfront, the Paulist Fathers opened the Seaman's Catholic Institute for the use of all seamen, without distinction of race, color, or creed. Two large rooms were provided with reading and writing materials, with games and other forms of entertainment. Weekly lectures on educational and religious subjects were provided. Letters were written for illiterate seamen and a mail service maintained. (106) The Catholic Seaman's Institute proved very popular and had an average daily attendance of more than one hundred. In January, 1902, the Institute was moved to the basement of Old St. Mary's Church so that the Fathers could devote more time to it. The facilities were destroyed in the earthquake and fire of 1906 and not reinstituted when the Church was rebuilt. Since 1933, this work has been cared for by the Apostleship of the Sea, with headquarters at 399 Fremont Street in San Francisco.

Further evidence of the increasing vitality of Old St. Mary's parish was the formation of Company "M" of the First Regiment, League of The Cross Cadets. This organization encouraged close participation in parish affairs by the young men of the parish and gave the young people a gymnasium and reading room. (107) For the young girls of the parish a free sewing school was opened in February, 1899. Under the direction of competent teachers it sought to teach skills in the most popular activity of young girls, fancy and useful sewing. (108)

Thus we see that, by the turn of the century, in six short years, Old St. Mary's under the vigorous direction of the Paulists had reached out to many elements of the Catholic population. Old St. Mary's had thrown off the grime of half a century: the Church itself was clean within and without and beautified by stained glass windows as well as decently lighted by electricity and its sanctuary was soon to be furnished with a new altar. Such material accomplishments would seem to be enough.

But the Paulists sought a spiritual revival. The physical building was merely a necessary step. The great work was to be of a spiritual nature. As we have mentioned, new religious sodalities were organized and old ones revived. Organizations for young men and young girls were active and flourishing. To a person looking back from the perspective afforded by fifty years it seems as if a miracle had taken place. In 1890, Archbishop Riordan was seriously considering abandoning Old St. Mary's for it seemed as if its usefulness was ended. A short ten years later the Paulist Fathers were in charge of one of the most active parishes, spiritually and materially, in San Francisco. It was a powerhouse for Catholicism. This venerable old stone Church was entering a new and greater era.

However, one menacing cloud hung over old St. Mary's. The Paulists faced two problems when they accepted this parish. The first was within their power to solve and they solved it. They had revived Old St. Mary's spiritually. They also sought to abolish the flagrant immorality thrusting its corrupt visage from every door and window that looked upon Old St. Mary's. Father Wyman stated this problem clearly in the December issue of the Paulist Calendar in 1897. He wrote:

A few words of explanation will doubtless prove interesting to those who have the city's welfare at heart, and wish to see suppressed a crime which has flaunted itself so openly in the faces of tourists and visitors, that they have left our fair city more affected by the evidences of its depravity than impressed by its scenes of beauty, and likewise to the lovers of Old St. Mary's, who have grieved on account of the blatant and blighting scandal which has confronted the Church so long and threatened to close the door which for over forty years has opened to admit God's children, that they might kneel in his presence.

Why this evil was permitted to grow up and flourish we cannot explain, but if the apathy of those formerly entrusted with the law equal the indifference of those who now hold the same trust, we need not go far to seek an explanation. When first we attempted to remove the evil from before our eyes we met with opposition from sources we did not

58

expect. "It is too bad the Church is there," expressed the consolation and sympathy offered by some. They seemed to think the Church ought to be removed in order that the violation of the law might meet with less interference or opposition.

"What are you going to do about it?" was the encouragement we received from others. We had to do something and so we did what we could. Though immorality is forbidden by the commandments, we knew arguments based on this reason would reach and affect only certain classes, and so we had recourse to the state law, which makes it a misdemeanor, punishable by fine or imprisonment or both, for owners or agents to rent houses for immoral purposes. We appealed to the police department to enforce this law. The newspapers of the city helped us in our struggle, and after a time, we succeeded in having Dupont Street made passable and were assured that a relegation to the upper stories would be insisted upon. But, in spite of our appeal, no action was taken against the other streets. They flourished in their wickedness and laughed us to scorn. They prospered so well that the number of apartments had to be increased at a cost of reduction in size and accommodation. It is but a few weeks since we were disturbed on Sunday morning by the sound of hammers and the clatter of boards. They cared not for Sunday in their feverish haste to multiply the dens of iniquity. Again, what could we do? We appealed to the Honorable Board of Supervisors, individually, and asked them to help us in our struggle for morality and decency. (109)

Father Wyman's effort to abolish the evil led him to ask that the "cribs" directly across from Old St. Mary's on California Street be torn down and a public park be built. With the aid of the newspapers, Mayor Phelan, The Board of Supervisors, and several members of the bench, Father Wyman vigorously campaigned for St. Mary's Square but the "cribs" remained. Neither law and order nor public indignation could make any headway against this corruption. The flimsy partitions of the "cribs" were buttressed by the money reaped from corruption and stood like a fortress against the forces of decency. But the evil men who defied decency for more than a decade reaped a whirlwind of heartbreak in three short days, for earthquake leveled the filth to the ground and then consumed it in the holocaust of fire. In a few short hours the abomination was destroyed forever. Four years later, in 1910, Father Wyman could joyously report:

We rejoice to inform our readers that St. Mary's Square is now an

59

accomplished fact. Who of us that remembers the moral plague spot there that once disgraced our whole city does not thank God that (it) is now removed forever. (110)

It is true that vice was driven out at a terrible cost in suffering and loss. But Old St. Mary's still stood, while the places of evil were gone.

As a Phoenix From the Ashes...

When the rumble of the earthquake, on the morning of April 18, 1906, had given way to silence which enshrouded the stricken city, Old St. Mary's Church stood solidly on its foundations, laid half a century ago. The great cross and pediment on the front of the tower had fallen, crushing the granite steps of the main entrance; two small finials surmounting side buttresses had also fallen, and a few delicate pinnacles of exquisitely carved Cararra marble had been broken from the Gothic altars within. Otherwise it was uninjured. The solemn orderliness, the soothing harmony of line and color, the quiet richness of artistic embellishment, characteristic of the old Church's interior, maintained the secular peace with which all who loved it were familiar, as the sacred edifice awaited the Holy Sacrifice of another day.

After noon, the battle lines of the fire, which had drifted away south of Market Street, were seen to reform and menace the old Cathedral. The priests and sacristan, anxious for the safety of the sacred books and vestments and vessels, hurriedly gathered them together and transported them to places of safety. Some, entrusted to a palace on Nob Hill, were afterwards destroyed, and in this fate was included the most beautiful and costly of all the vestments. But the greater portion were carried several miles away and were saved.

Then the custodians of Old St. Mary's devoted the remainder of the day to frantic effort, based on hope of protecting the Church from fire. They made use of every known device of fire fighting, and for a few hours they were sanguine of success. Suddenly the hose flattened in the hands of the brave men on the roof, and shortly after they had made the heartbreaking discovery that not another drop of water was available for use in any manner, the soldiers came and compelled them to desert their post. Before midnight the sea of fire swept over the entire district, and Old St. Mary's had burned gloriously, sending up a last column of flame high in heaven from the open top of its venerable tower.

After the ruins had cooled and the restrictions of martial law had been relaxed, the Church was carefully examined by expert architects.

60

The parochial residence was a forlorn shell of dilapidated walls, broken in many places, and so dangerous that it was razed to the ground by command of the municipality. But the church, with the exception of the rear gable, was marvelously intact. Everything inflammable had, of course, been consumed. The sweet toned bell lay on the dome of the vestibule in scattered lumps of melted metal. A few rust-eaten parts of the electric motor alone recalled the new grand organ. The marble side altars, imported from Italy, and recently consecrated, had melted like wax; only a carved bunch of grapes and a little, legless lamb from the Bethlehem panel remaining as relics. The main altar, perhaps the most perfect specimen of Cararra marble, was reduced entirely to dust and lost in the ashes. One piece of glass representing a human foot, from the group picturing the conversion of St. Paul, was actually the sole remainder of the magnificent stained windows with which the Church had been equipped a few years before.

In spite of such evidences of a holocaust, the foundations and walls of the Church, laid and erected in devout faith and simple honesty over fifty years ago, were not only uninjured by crack or disintegration, but the experts declared that it would require fully a third of the original cost to demolish them, and their reproduction under present conditions would be practically impossible. (111)

This was the bleak prospect that faced Father Wyman. The work and effort of more than a decade had been wiped out overnight. The flourishing parish of Old St. Mary's was gone. For more than a mile on every side of the church the city lay desolated. Nothing remained of the Church but the four walls. The parish house was completely razed. From Market Street to Jackson Street, from Davis Street to Jones Street, the actual limits of the parish, whatever structures had not been tumbled down by the earthquake had been consumed by the subsequent flames. How could anyone stand on the shattered steps of Old St. Mary's with desolation on every side and hope that once again this building could be one of the great spiritual centers of the city of St. Francis.

In the heart of one man this hope was bright and strong. As soon as the possibility of reconstruction was confirmed by critical examination and tests, Father Wyman urged that the Church be rebuilt. But he stood alone. The Paulists in New York thought otherwise. Archbishop Riordan was not convinced that to rebuild on the old location was the wise thing to do. Father Wyman argued and prayed. He had seen a spiritual rebirth in ten years. Could not a physical rebirth be more easily achieved?

Meanwhile the people needed the Mass and the Sacraments. Father Wyman built a temporary church on the site of the former parish house. This building was used at first only for Divine services and the fathers lived in a house on Pine near Webster until February, 1907. These were the darkest days for Old St. Mary's. How could Father Wyman think of rebuilding the church when even the temporary wooden church could not be filled. Father James P. Towey (1882-   ) recalls:

From a mere handful of people gradually the number grew in the little wooden church which was built on the site of the rectory. I remember preaching to a mere handful of people and of going out to the little temporary church on Sunday nights to recite the Rosary with only one man to answer — one whom I suspected was there not because of devotion but because it offered temporary shelter from the weather. (112)

In February, 1907, the Paulists took up their residence in quarters prepared in the temporary church building. Now more than ever Father Wyman worked for rebuilding Old St. Mary's. He wrote to a friend concerning his hope to rebuild, "If Old St. Mary's is not to be rebuilt, then my heart will be buried deep in the ruins." (113)

Such conviction in the future greatness of Old St. Mary's could not be denied. By April, 1908, the approval to rebuild had been granted and Father Wyman could announce:

The plans for the restoration and rebuilding of our Church are now being studied most carefully and as soon as their durability and the cost of their execution can be properly estimated the work will begin. (114)

The plans, finally approved, called for the reconstruction of the Church along the former lines. The construction was under the direction of Thomas J. Welsh, a prominent San Francisco architect. The cost of rebuilding the Church would be fifty thousand dollars. This did not include the plastering or any Church furnishings. The insurance money paid for the loss of the Church in 1906 was forty-seven thousand dollars.

On Sunday, June 20, 1909, at 10:30 A.M., Old St. Mary's was dedicated by Archbishop Riordan to the service of God. The Paulist Fathers could again begin the task of restoring Old St. Mary's as the spiritual powerhouse. But the other great problem, the vice infested district, was gone forever. In the words announcing the dedication, the Paulist Fathers happily stated:

The location has greatly improved during the period of rebuilding; the low and vicious resorts which once were in this vicinity have been obliterated forever. (115)

Since the Church was rebuilt in 1909, the Paulists have added greatly to the size, beauty, and usefulness of Old St. Mary's. But this has been done without modifying the familiar lines of the Church so dear to the hearts of the people of San Francisco. The temporary church on the site of the rectory was named Alemany Hall and served as an auditorium until a new rectory was built on the site. A grand reception for all the friends of Old St. Mary's was held in the basement of the rectory August 9, 1910, to mark the completion of the new parish house.

In April, 1925, the Paulist Fathers commenced improvements on the Church. Seating capacity, through rearrangement of the interior, was increased from seven hundred to thirteen hundred. A new heating and ventilating system were installed and property on grant Avenue, just back of the sanctuary wall, was purchased for $60,000. The improvements cost an additional $35,000 and were completed in September, 1925. In September, 1928, the rectory was enlarged by the addition of another floor, and the installation of an elevator. The windows of the parish house were altered to conform more closely to the architecture of the Church.

Some details of the furnishings of the Church may be mentioned here. The beautiful paintings over the High Altar are copies of the famous Immaculate Conception of Murillo, and St. Michael and the Annunciation by Guido Reni, made at Rome by Amando Vandelli. These paintings were donated by Frank J. Sullivan in 1911. The High Altar was consecrated on January 23, 1911. By special permission of the Most Reverend Archbishop, the ceremony of consecration was performed by Father Wyman, assisted by Father Woodman. The Saints whose relics are preserved in the Altar are Saints Jucundinus and Blandinus, Martyrs.

In January, 1929, major alterations of the Church structure were begun. The sanctuary and sacristy were extended over the property purchased on Grant Avenue and an East transept added to the main body of the Church. These alterations cost $150,000, and they were major improvements for the old Church. The building was extended in length nearly fifty feet and the seating capacity increased to two thousand. As part of the expansion a new parish hall was built beneath the Church. This hall was opened on October 11, 1929. These major improvements were completed in time for the celebration of the Diamond Jubilee of Old St. Mary's Church. The services of the Diamond Jubilee were opened on December 1, 1929, by the Reverend John B. Harney (1875-   ), Superior General of the Paulist Fathers, who preached two sermons, one in the morning and one in the evening. The closing services of the Jubilee witnessed a Pontifical Mass celebrated by Bishop John J. Mitty of Salt Lake City, Utah, with Archbishop Edward J. Hanna presiding and Pontifical Benediction in the evening.

Thus, we see that God has blessed the work of the Paulists at Old St. Mary's in San Francisco. Improvements to the Church, rectory, and Catholic Chinese mission totaled over half a million dollars. But great as this material improvement may be, it is nothing if not accompanied by a greater spiritual growth. To understand how fire blackened walls could be turned into a church seating nearly three times its original capacity and representing an investment in capital improvements of more than half a million dollars one must look to the equally tremendous spiritual growth of the parish.

To fully describe the growth of each activity of the Paulist Fathers would be far beyond the scope of this work. We can merely indicate the nature of this tremendous outpouring of zeal and effort by indicating the early and rapid revival of parish activities after the earthquake and fire and the present multitiple activities of the parish.

In order to integrate the work of the Paulists and the members of Old St. Mary's parish, immediate steps were taken to reorganize organizations for all age groups. In November, 1910, St. Mary's Boys Club for the youth of the parish was organized. In January, 1911, the Alemany Club, a religious and social club for young men of the parish was established. The Holy Name Society was organized June 14, 1911. The Catholic Truth Society was reorganized in August, 1911, under the direction of the Paulists. The League of the Cross Cadets was reorganized March 25, 1911. St. Mary's Court No. 964, Women's Catholic Order of Foresters was instituted September 4, 1911. St. Anthony's Guild was established on October 15,

1911. This is but a partial list of the renewed life of the parish shortly after Old St. Mary's was rebuilt.

Before concluding this brief story of the work of the Paulist Fathers during the years 1894-1951 at San Francisco, we must point out several activities of the Paulists which cannot be passed over without a few words.

One of the great works of the Paulists has been the formation of societies of young people for social and religious activities. This work began in January, 1911, with the formation of the Alemany Club, named after the Prelate who had built Old St. Mary's Church. This club was organized for Catholic young men. It secured club rooms at 418 Montgomery Street and planned to meet on the second and fourth Thursday of each month. On June 14, 1911, the Holy Name Society was organized in Old St. Mary's parish and gradually absorbed the Alemany Club since the purpose of both was much the same.

It was not until November, 1940, that plans for a society of young men and women was again revived. Father Paul Ward (1894-1951) outlined the framework for his proposed group. It was to be for younger people of the parish, especially the recent alumni of various colleges and high schools, in the hope that they would meet together for the discussion of the questions of the day; to meet other young Catholic people; to obtain a more firm grasp upon the priceless gift of their faith.

Shortly afterwards, the group took the name of the Wyman Club honoring Father Henry Harrison Wyman. From the first this parish activity flourished. James Bacigalupi was named president and Margaret Beck secretary. On January 8, 1941, the membership had grown so rapidly that reorganization with delegation of duties to a complete staff of officers was felt necessary. Martin Mahoney, active in Old St. Mary's young people's activities, was elected president to succeed James Bacigalupi, who refused re-election.

The members of the Wyman Club frequently sponsored dances and other entertainment for service men. In July, 1941, before the outbreak of the war, the Wyman Club initiated a series of dances every other Friday evening for members of the armed forces. (116)

The Wyman Club continued active until 1944. With most of

the young men in the service, it was felt that these young men needed the facilities which Old St. Mary's could offer. On March 17, 1944, Father Thomas Burke (1871-1947), the pastor of Old St. Mary's, and Father John J. Dimond (1916-   ), Director of Old St. Mary's Service Center, opened the doors and facilities of the Center to all service men and women. With the shortage of skilled labor and other war time difficulties confronting him, it was necessary for Father Dimond together with Father William Mc-Donald (1904-   ) to prepare the facilities of the auditorium beneath the Church with their own hands. Recruiting the help of service men, Fathers Dimond and McDonald worked fourteen hours a day to finish the renovation. Walls were plastered and painted to turn store rooms into a kitchen and cloak room. Electrical and plumbing equipment was installed; floors scrubbed, waxed, and polished; woodwork painted, windows washed, and drapes hung before anyone could start thinking of this large auditorium as a "home away from home." Yet, this is the one phrase that came best to describe the atmosphere of Old St. Mary's Service Center — "Home." With the end of hostilities and the return of service men and women to their homes, the need for a service center ceased. But during the months from March 17, 1944, to the date the Center closed, September 15, 1946, four hundred fifty thousand service men and women had visited their "home away from home."

The facilities of the Center were soon utilized to serve an equally vital need during the post war period. In January, 1948, Old St. Mary's Center was organized by Father Edward Lawler (1916-   ). The aim of the Center Program is to provide a religious and cultural background for a social and recreational program of interest to young men and women, single or married, to guide them in bringing the advantages of Catholic culture to the business and social world of the day.

The Catholic Chinese Mission ...

In 1894, the Paulist Fathers came from the East to take over the administration of Old St. Mary's Church; and a short eight years later in 1902, one of its priests sowed the first seeds for the only Catholic mission for the Chinese in America. After the Paulist Fathers and their General Council approved the idea of establishing this mission, a young Paulist priest, Reverend Henry I. Stark (1880-1946), a native San Franciscan, was chosen to begin this

66

newest Paulist apostolate. The young priest had a difficult time in getting started because the Chinese were at that time none too friendly toward Americans on account of persecution at the hands of American laborers who resented the cheap wages for which they were willing to work. Father Stark first met with opposition and indifference; but finally, through persistent efforts, broke through their distrust. He opened a Sunday School in the basement of Old St. Mary's where he taught English. In the year 1904, Father Stark was offered new quarters, a little community house on Howard Street, chiefly through the efforts of Mrs. Bertha Welch. Mrs. Welch and a Mrs. Ella Clemmons, a non-Catholic who later became a convert to Catholicism, thought the work would progress faster if several nuns who could speak Chinese were attached to the school. The plan was approved by Archbishop Riordan with the result that the Helpers of the Holy Souls were invited to the diocese, among whom were two native Chinese Sisters, Mother St. Ida and Mother St. Rose.

Not long after this, a house on Clay Street above Stockton Street was procured for the use of the Mission, the largest place until then. The following year the two Chinese Sisters opened a kindergarten class with Mrs. Clemmons helping as house mother. This little Mission progressed and the little school became popular with the Chinese people. Then, two years later, in April, 1906 came the devastating earthquake and fire, with it the little Mission was destroyed.

With the rapid rebuilding of San Francisco, the Chinese also reestablished themselves, but it was not until 1909 that Father Stark could make another beginning, back in the basement of Old St. Mary's. Chinatown had about 15,000 inhabitants at this time. Father Stark, because other priestly duties demanded much of his attention, gave up his Mission work in 1910 and was succeeded by Father Charles Bradley (1876-1947).

The first thing Father Bradley did was to look for a suitable place inside Chinatown for housing the Mission. He found an empty store on Clay Street and began teaching his classes. From 1911 to 1920, St. Mary's was quite a mobile Mission with Father Bradley trying repeatedly to find a permanent location without success. Finally Mrs. Bertha Welch promised to finance the building of a large edifice if Father Bradley could find the proper site.

This he did, and on August 1, 1921, the present Chinese Mission at 902 Stockton Street was opened for all the Chinese. The services of six sisters of St. Joseph of Orange were obtained to conduct the grades of the new elementary school.

The first religious fruits of the Mission after the permanent building was erected occurred on January 9, 1922, when fifty Chinese were received into the Church through Baptism. Grade classes were taught between 9 A.M. and 3 P.M. in the elementary school; then from 5 P.M. to 9 P.M., Chinese language classes were held, taught by Chinese teachers, as well as English classes taught by volunteer American teachers.

Between 1922 and 1926 the attendance at the school and at Sunday services increased steadily. Scores of converts were baptized each year. Young people's clubs were organized — athletic, dramatic, music, dancing, etc., until the Mission was so packed that Father Bradley finally had to enlarge it. This was done by adding an entire new floor to the building. In addition, an adjoining three-story building was purchased as a convent for the Sisters of St. Joseph. This new building Father Bradley financed with a great Chinese Festival, Faii Dong Wu or the Feast of the Lanterns, in February, 1927. People from all over San Francisco participated and it grossed all of $25,000.

By 1927, the Mission was still steadily expanding in all its activities, and more than 1,000 Chinese had become Catholics and more were receiving instructions. Father Bradley, however, after seventeen years of continuous labor at the Mission was a tired man — and was transferred to another Paulist Mission in the East, being succeeded by a young Paulist, Father Peter Bergen (1904). Father Bergen organized dental and social service activities in addition to continuing all the projects of Father Bradley. In 1929, when the depression started, Father Bergen also organized an Auxiliary Corps, an organization of American Catholics and non-Catholics, who aided the Mission financially and physically. Today this Auxiliary is a veritable backbone of the Mission, numbering about 1,500 members. Through the dental clinic, the first of its kind in Chinatown, over 500 children of St. Mary's were examined for dental defects during the first few years of operation.

The Social Service Bureau started by Father Bergen secured hospitalization for the sick, work for the unemployed, and help for the needy ones through the proper agencies for direct and work relief. Immigration and juvenile delinquency cases were also handled. Through the unselfish work of this Bureau, Chinatown came to have a great admiration and respect for St. Mary's and for the Catholic religion. Another work initiated by Father Bergen was lunch service for the school children.

In 1932, because of ill health, Father Bergen was forced to relinquish his post as director of the Mission and was succeeded by Father George Johnson (1904-   ), from Chicago. Under Father Johnson's guidance, all the religious, social and educational works of the Mission were continued, improved and, wherever possible, expanded. Attendance in day and evening schools increased. A special music class was inaugurated — the first of its kind in Chinatown, and later the beginning of a large Girls' Drum Corps. In 1933 the first Chinese Court of the Catholic Daughters of America was established.

Father Johnson guided the Mission successfully through the depression, from which it emerged not only as a recognized and highly respected Christian Mission, with an excellent English and Chinese School, but as a well organized social center. Father Johnson was succeeded in 1939 by Father Charles Donovan (1915-   ), who carried on the various activities during the rugged years of World War II — and kept all the organizations flourishing, although the social service work was discontinued in part because of the Government's closing of W.P.A. activity.

In 1947, Father Donovan was succeeded by Father Donal F. Forrester (1906-   ), the present Director, who has been particularly active in encouraging athletics and sports among the young people, as well as fostering many social activities among both old and young. Boy Scouts, Cub Scouts, Campfire Girls, Bluebirds — all have been added to the other organizations. While the Holy Name Society, Catholic War Veterans, St. Mary's Parent-Teachers Group, have all been reactivated during his administration of the Mission's affairs. St. Mary's Girls' Drum corps, Girls' Drill Team, Majorettes, (the last two added during the past few years) have received expert instruction and are much in demand not only in California but in many outside States for appearances at civic celebrations, etc. For young people between the ages of 18 and 30 there is the Apostolati Society. The Boys' Club which has functioned for many years, is still most active, both junior and senior members

69

and alumni. The Boys' Basketball Team, as well as the Girls' Basketball Team are in the various city tournaments (C.Y.O., Examiner, etc.) and a Tennis Club is also active. Newest organization is the Glee Club, for both boys and girls, which has appeared several times in public, as well as on Television and Radio Broadcasts — and which staged its first Operetta at the Mission, October 20, 1951. (117)

Other Paulist Activities — Old St. Mary's ...

No account of the Paulists' work in any parish would be complete without a mention of two activities which are of special interest to the Paulists.

The first activity is the conversion of non-Catholics. The first formal class for non-Catholics who were interested in learning more concerning the Catholic Church was begun in April, 1898. As a result of a mission to non-Catholics, a class of inquiry was instituted at its close, so that the general truths discussed during the mission would find more personal and immediate application to the non-Catholics. Since that time regular classes have been held at Old St. Mary's for all persons interested in seeking the true and complete doctrine of the Catholic Church.

At the present time (1951) classes of inquiry are held twice a week in the lecture room of the Paulist Library of Old St. Mary's. These classes are being conducted by Fathers Martin J. O'Looney (1918-   ), and Joseph A. Burns (1911-   ). Of those taking classes of inquiry, in recent years, approximately 200 non-Catholics have embraced Catholicism annually.

The second great work of the Paulists in San Francisco has been the establishment of the Paulist Circulating Library. On October 6, 1930, the Paulist Circulating Library was established. At present there are more than 6,000 volumes available to all those interested in current and Catholic literature. An unusual and most praiseworthy activity of the Paulist Library has been the efforts of Father Claude J. Collins (1907-   ), who since 1947 has been the Pastor of Old St. Mary's, to secure as guest speakers men and women prominent in the life of San Francisco and in national affairs. Outstanding Catholic and non-Catholic leaders in every walk of life have presented their views on current and controversial issues. During the month of October, 1951, in two series of lectures, the Paulist Forum presented nationally renowned speakers on current events affecting the Catholic viewpoint. Dr. Mortimer Adler spoke on "The Hundred Great Ideas" while the Catholic Attitude Series presented the District Attorney of San Francisco, Mr. Thomas J. Lynch, who spoke on "Organized Crime."

In summing up the history of Old St. Mary's as a Paulist parish one central theme remains the keynote of the whole picture. The courage and confidence of Father Wyman as he looked upon the blackened walls of Old St. Mary's on April 19, 1906, remains. The purpose he established as his goal — to build Old St. Mary's Church into a spiritual dynamo enlightening and enlivening the lives of all within its reach — remains. Throughout the history of Old St. Mary's as a Paulist parish new and permanent contributions to Catholicism had their beginnings in this First Cathedral in California. The Newman Club movement on university campuses was begun by the Paulist Fathers at the University of California, Berkeley Campus, August 15, 1907. The introduction of noon-day Mass for working people was suggested by the priests of Old St. Mary's. The daily Exposition of the Blessed Sacrament with Rosary and Benediction at 5:15 is offered for the working Catholics of the downtown district of San Francisco. The Three Hours Devotion on Good Friday at Old St. Mary's has become an outstanding feature of San Francisco Catholic life. Several thousand persons unable to enter Old St. Mary's reverently listen in St. Mary's Square to the service by means of a public address system. The Paulist Fathers have served as Catholic chaplains of the City Prison and County Jail located within their parochial limits.

To some the work of Old St. Mary's as a Paulist parish may seem spectacular. But it is spectacular in the same sense as Old St. Mary's was when it was dedicated as the Cathedral on California Street on Christmas Day, 1854. In a town largely composed of tents and temporary dwellings, the largest building in San Francisco was the new Cathedral. But the strength and permanency of the work of Old St. Mary's will be as the Church itself, unshaken by earthquake and fire, rising from adversity to new and greater stature.

ARCHBISHOPS OF SAN FRANCISCO

Most Reverend Joseph Sadoc Alemany, O.P., D.D.
1853 to 1884

Most Reverend Patrick William Riordan, D.D.
1884-1914

Most Reverend Edward Joseph Hanna, D.D.
1914-1935

Most Reverend John Joseph Mitty, D.D.
1935-

PASTORS OF OLD ST. MARY'S

Rev. Hugh P. Gallagher - - - - - - - 1854 - 1861

Rev. James Croke - - - - - - - 1861 - 1871

Rev. John J. Prendergast - - - - - - - 1871 - 1891

Rev. John J. Sullivan - - - - - - - 1891 - 1892

Rev. Thomas Larkin - - - - - - - 1892 - 1894

Rev. Edward Brady, C.S.P. - - - - - - 1894 - 1895

Rev. Henry H. Wyman, C.S.P. - - - - - 1895 - 1901

Rev. Michael P. Smith, C.S.P. - - - - - 1901 - 1904

Rev. Henry H. Wyman, C.S.P. - - - - - 1904 - 1910

Rev. Thomas J. Cullen, C.S.P. - - - - - 1910 - 1917

Rev. Michael P. Smith, C.S.P. - - - - - 1917 - 1919

Rev. William J. Cartwright, C.S.P. - - - - 1919 - 1922

Rev. Edward T. Mallon, C.S.P. - - - - - 1922 - 1928

Rev. Thomas F. Burke, C.S.P. - - - - - 1928 - 1934

Rev. James P. Towey, C.S.P. - - - - - 1934 - 1940

Rev. Wilfred G. Hurley, C.S.P. - - - - - 1940 - 1943

Rev. Thomas F. Burke, C.S.P. - - - - - 1943 - 1947

Rev. Claude J. Collins, C.S.P. - - - - - 1947 -

BIBLIOGRAPHY

Bibliographical Guides ...

Beers, Henry P. *Bibliographies in American History,* with a Guide to Materials for Research. (New York, 1942) Pages 222-223 list materials for church history.

Bepler, Doris W. "Descriptive Catalogue of Materials for Western History in California Magazines, 1854-1890." (M. A. thesis, University of California, 1920). Contains a subject index to articles which appear in *The Pioneer, Hutchings California Magazine, The Pacific Monthly, Overland Monthly* (1st and 2nd Series), *The Californian,* and *Golden Era.*

Chapman, Charles E. *A History of California, The Spanish Period* (New York, 1921) Contains an annotated bibliography of Spanish and American periods of California history.

Cowan, Robert E. *Bibliography of the History of California and the Far West.* (San Francisco, 1914) This is an annotated and critical bibliography of about a thousand printed works. It contains author and subject index.

............, *Bibliography of California,* 1510-1930. (3 v. San Francisco, 1930) This contains a listing of nearly every printed work dealing with California. It is not critical as is his earlier one volume bibliography referred to above.

Coy, Owen Cochran. *Guide to the County Archives of California.* (Sacramento, 1919) Does not index individual documents but sketches each county archive and lists important sub-groups of documents preserved.

Ellis, John T. *A Select Bibliography of the History of the Catholic Church in the United States.* (New York, 1947).

Guide to Depositories of Manuscript Collections in the United States: California. The Southern California Historical Records Survey Project (Los Angeles, California, 1941) This is a listing of the documents or groups of documents in public and private collections or archives in the State of California and a partial list of such documents in archives outside the state of California.

San Francisco Newspapers..

San Francisco Alta California
San Francisco Chronicle
San Francisco Daily Evening Bulletin
San Francisco Daily Morning Call
San Francisco Examiner
San Francisco Herald and Mirror

San Francisco Catholic Newspapers...

San Francisco Guardian (1858-1862)
San Francisco Monitor (1857-Present)

Other Catholic Newspapers...

New York Freeman's Journal (1840-1918)
New York Catholic Review (1872-1889)
Cincinnati Catholic Telegraph (1831-present)
Baltimore Catholic Mirror (1849-1908)

California Magazines...

Golden Era
Grizzly Bear
Hutchings California Magazine
Californian
Overland Monthly (1st and 2nd Series)
Pioneer
Pacific Monthly

Catholic Magazines...

Catholic World
American Catholic Quarterly Review
Brownson's Review

General Histories of California...

Bancroft, Hubert Howe. *Works* (39 v. San Francisco, 1882-1891)
Volumes 18 to 24 *History of California*
Volume 34 *California Pastoral*
Volume 35 *California Inter Pocula*

Eldredge, Zoeth Skinner. *History of California* (5 v. New York, 1915) A general History of California following the lines of Bancroft and Hittell. Volume 5 contains monographs on special topics of California History by contributors. There are few citations of source material.

Hittell, Theodore. *History of California.* (4 v. San Francisco, Vols. I, II, 1885; Vols. III, IV, 1897) Fails to recognize the part played by the Catholic Church in California History. From this defect his history fails by omission.

Royce, Josiah. *California, from the conquest in 1846 to the second Vigilance committee in San Francisco; a study of American character.* (Boston and New York, 1886) As indicated in the title the author limits his treatment to the years 1846-1856. He also adopts a special viewpoint from which he develops his history; namely, a critical study of the men in California at this time.

Tuthill, Franklin. *The History of California* (San Francisco, 1866) A valuable report inasmuch as it was written by a man who was contemporary with much that he reported.

General Histories of San Francisco

The Bay of San Francisco, the Metropolis of the Pacific Coast and its Suburban Cities (2 v. Chicago, 1892)

Byington, Lewis F. and Lewis, Oscar. *The History of San Francisco* (3 v. Chicago, 1931)

Eldredge, Zoeth Skinner. *The Beginnings of San Francisco from the Expedition of Anza 1774, to the city charter of April 15, 1850* (2 v. San Francisco, 1912) Actually this work deals almost completely with the Spanish period in California. Less than one-fourth of the pages deal with San Francisco History.

Hittell, John Shertzer. *A History of the City of San Francisco and Incidentally of the State of California* (San Francisco, 1878) Deliberately minimizes the work and influence of the missionaries. Neglects the important contribution of religion in American Period.

Millard, Bailey. *History of the San Francisco Bay Region* (3 v. San Francisco, 1924)

Young, John Philip. *San Francisco, a History of the Pacific Metropolis* (2 v. San Francisco, 1912)

Histories of the Catholic Church and Religious Groups . . .

Anthony, Sister M. *In Harvest Fields By Sunset Shores* (San Francisco, 1926) A valuable study of the coming and early history of the Sisters of Notre Dame in California.

Clinch, Bryan. *California and Its Missions: Their History to the Treaty of Guadalupe Hidalgo* (2 v. San Francisco, 1904) The author is just in evaluating the work and purpose of the missions in California. He condemns the exploitation and ruin of the mission system.

Conmy, Peter T. "A History of St. Francis Parish." An unpublished manuscript tracing the history of the parish from 1849 to 1949 and valuable for the beginning of American Catholicism in California.

Dehey, Elinor T. *Religious Orders of Women in U. S.* (Hammond, Indiana, 1913)

Engelhardt, Zephyrin. *Missions and Missionaries of California* (4 v. San Francisco, 1908-1915) A very valuable study of the entire mission system and early California Catholic History. He has made extensive use of the source material and his conclusions are justified by these materials. At times he defends the work of the missionaries rather than recounts it.

Geary, Rev. Gerald. "Transfer of Ecclesiastical Jurisdiction in California, 1840-1853." Catholic Historical Society, Historical Records and Studies, XXII, 1932.

..........., *The Secularization of the California Missions,* 1810-1846 (Washington, D.C., 1934)

Herron, Sister Mary Eulalia. *The Sisters of Mercy in the United States* (New York, 1929)

Kavanagh, Rev. D. J., S. J. *Holy Family Sisters of San Francisco* (San Francisco, 1922) A valuable study of this order of Sisters which was founded in San Francisco in 1878.

Presentation Sisters, San Francisco (no author indicated) *Oak Leaves, 1854-1904* (San Francisco—no date) One of the earliest Orders of Sisters to come to California—essential to the story of Archbishop Alemany.

O'Gormon, Thomas. *History of The Roman Catholic Church in U. S.* (4th ed. New York, 1907)

Riordan, Rev. Joseph W., S.J. *The First Half Century of St. Ignatius Church and College* (San Francisco, 1905)

Shea, John G. *History of the Catholic Church in U. S. From 5th Provincial Council to 2nd Plenary Council of Baltimore* (4 Vols., New York, 1892)

Thomas, P. J. *Memoir of Mother Mary Teresa Comerford* (San Francisco, 1882)

..........., *Our Centennial Memoir* (San Francisco, 1877)

Walsh, Henry L., S. J. *Hallowed Were the Gold Dust Trails* (Santa Clara, California, 1946) This is an excellent treatment of the colorful story of pioneer priests during the gold rush days of California. It indicates the need of full length biographies of many of the men who must, of necessity, be treated sketchily.

Directories, Annals, and Abstracts ...

Code, Joseph B. *Dictionary of the American Hierarchy* (New York, 1940)

Hanna, Philip Townsend. *California Through Four Centuries, a Handbook of Memorable Dates.* (New York, 1935)

Huggins, Dorothy H. *Continuation of the Annals of San Francisco* (San Francisco, 1939)

Kimball, Charles P. (editor) *The San Francisco City Directory for 1850* (San Francisco, 1850)

Langley, H. G. (editor) (other editors later) *The San Francisco Directory and Business Guide* (San Francisco, 1863, et. seq.)

Shearer, Donald C., O.F.M. *Pontificia Americana; A Documentary History of the Catholic Church in the United States, 1784-1884* (Washington, D.C., 1933) A valuable reference work.

Shuck, Oscar Tully. *Historical Abstract of San Francisco* (3 v. San Francisco, 1897) Although three volumes were planned only volume one was completed.

Soule, Frank, Gihon, John H., and Nesbet, James. *The Annals of San Francisco* . . . (New York, 1855) Fails to give the Catholic Church the prominence it rightfully deserved in these early days.

California and the Civil War ...

Ellison, Joseph. *California and the Nation 1846-1869* (Berkeley, 1927)

Kennedy, Elijah R. *Contest for California in 1861* (Boston, 1912)

Murphy, Robert P. "Catholic Church in the United States during the Civil War—1852-1866." American Catholic Historical Society, Philadelphia *Records* XXXIX, December 1928.

General Biographies...

Altrocchi, Julia C. *The Spectacular San Franciscans* (New York, 1949)

Bancroft, Hubert Howe. *Chronicles of the Builders of the Commonwealth* (7 v. and index, San Francisco, 1891-1898)

Blake, Evarts I. (editor). *San Francisco a Brief Biographical Sketch of Some of the Most Prominent Men* (San Francisco, 1902)

Clarke, Richard H. *Lives of the Deceased Bishops of the Catholic Church in the United States* (New York, 1888)

Johnson, Allen, and Malone, Dumas (editors). *Dictionary of American Biography* (21 v., index, supplementary volume, New York, 1926-1944)

McGuire, Constantine (editor). *Catholic Builders of the Nation* (5 v. Boston, 1923)

Phelps, Alonzo. *Contemporary Biography of California's Representative Men* (San Francisco, 1881-1882)

Prendergast, Thomas E. *Forgotten Pioneers: Irish Leaders in Early California* (San Francisco, 1942)

Quigley, Rev. Hugh. *The Irish Race in California and on the Pacific Coast* (San Francisco, 1878) An interesting but not critical work.

San Francisco: Its Builders Past and Present, . . . (San Francisco, 1913)

Shuck, Oscar Tully. *Sketches of the Leading and Representative Men of San Francisco* (San Francisco, 1875)

Swasey, William F. *Early Days and Men of California* (Oakland, 1891)

Individual Biographies and Autobiographies...

Brennan, Thomas. "Archbishop Riordan." American Catholic Historical Society, Philadelphia Records XXVI, 1915.

Davis, William H. *Seventy-five Years in California* (San Francisco, 1929) Preceded by the author's *Sixty Years in California.*

Graves, Jackson. *My Seventy Years in California, 1857-1927* (Los Angeles, 1927)

Gray, Sister Gertrude Mary. "A Preliminary Survey of the Life of the Most Reverend Joseph Sadoc Alemany, O. P. First Bishop of San Francisco." M. A. Thesis, Catholic University of America, 1942. This study is a valuable contribution to the history of the Catholic Church in the early American Period.

Lynch, Jeremiah. *A Senator of the Fifties David C. Broderick of California.* (San Francisco, 1911)

Lyons, Sister Letitia Mary. *Francis Norbett Blanchet and the Founding of the Oregon Missions, 1838-1857* (Washington, D.C., 1940)

McGloin, John Bernard, S.J. *Eloquent Indian: The Life of James Bouchard California Jesuit* (Stanford University, 1949) This book is a major contribution to the history of the Catholic Church in California. It is only fitting that a priest of the stature of James Chrysostom Bouchard, S.J., one of the most famous clergymen in San Francisco seventy-five years ago, should be made known to this generation through this excellent biography.

Revere, James W. *A Tour of Duty in California . . .* (New York, 1849)

Root, Henry. *Personal History and Reminiscences With Personal Opinions on Contemporary Events 1845-1921* (San Francisco, 1921)

Snead-Cox, John George. *Life of Cardinal Vaughan* (2 v. London, 1910)

Taylor, Reverend William. *The Story of My Life* (New York, 1895)

Thomas, Sister Mary, O. P. *Apostle of the Valley; the Life of Daniel Francis Dade, Pioneer Priest of the San Joaquin Valley* (Fresno, 1947)

Willey, Reverend Samuel H. *Thirty Years in California, 1849-1879* (San Francisco, 1879)

Reminiscences, Sketches, and Descriptions . . .

Bari, Valeska. *The Course of Empire* (New York, 1931) First hand accounts of California during gold rush days of '49.

Barry, T. A., and Patten B. A. *Men and Memories of San Francisco in the Spring of 1850* (San Francisco, 1873)

Brewer, William H. *Up and Down California in 1860-1864* (New Haven, 1930)

Brown, John Henry. *Reminiscences and Incidents of the Early Days of San Francisco—Actual Experiences of an Eye-Witness, 1845-1850* (San Francisco, 1933)

Burnett, Peter. *Recollections and Opinions of an Old Pioneer* (New York, 1880) As former Governor of California and a convert to the Catholic Church, his opinions of early California life are a valuable commentary.

Bryant, Edwin. *What I Saw in California . . . in the Years 1846-1847.* (Santa Ana, California, 1936)

Camp, William M. *San Francisco Port of Gold* (New York, 1947)

Colton, Walter. *Three Years in California* (New York, 1856) Later edition, 1860, under title of. *The Land of Gold.*

Coulter, J. M. *Adventures on the West Coast of South America and the Interior of California* (London, 1847) Chapters 14-16 describe Mission Dolores of San Francisco.

Delano, Alonzo. *Pen Knife Sketches or Chips off the Old Block. A series of Original Illustrated Letters, Written by One of California's Pioneer Miners . . .* (Sacramento, 1853)

Earle, A. G. *Bringing In The Sheaves* (Boston, 1868)

Evans, Albert. *A La California: Sketches of Life in the Golden State* (San Francisco, 1873)

Ferrier, W. W. *Pioneer Church Beginnings and Educational Movements in California* (Berkeley, 1927)

Hammond, Reverend E. P. *Rev. E. P. Hammond's Eight Weeks in San Francisco* (San Francisco, 1875)

Helper, Minton R. *The Land of Gold: Reality Versus Fiction* (Baltimore, 1855)

Hunt, Rockwell D. *California the Golden* (San Francisco, 1911)

Jackson, Joseph H. *San Francisco Murders* (New York, 1947)

Jacobson, Pauline. *City of the Golden Fifties* (Berkeley, 1941)

Lloyd, Benjamin E. *Lights and Shades in San Francisco* (San Francisco, 1786)

Marryat, Frank. *Mountains and Molehills, or Recollections from a Burnt Journal* (London and New York, 1855)

Marye, George T. *From '49 to '83 in California and Nevada* (San Francisco, 1923)

MacMinn, George R. *Theater of the Golden Era in California,* (Caldwell, Idaho, 1941)

Neville, Amelia. *The Fantastic City* (New York, 1932)

Nordhof, Charles. *Northern California, Oregon, and the Sandwich Islands* (New York, 1874)

Player-Frowd, J. G. *Six Months in California* (London, 1872)

Prieto, Guillermo. *San Francisco in the Seventies* . . . (edited by Edwin S. Morby, San Francisco, 1938)

Robinson, Alfred. *Life in California* . . . (New York, 1846) The author of this book wrote an excellent account of the mission system as he saw it in California.

Sherman, Gen. William T. *Recollections of California 1845-1861* (Oakland, 1945)

Shuck, Oscar Tully. *California Scrapbook, a Repository of Useful Information and Select Readings; compiled by Oscar T. Shuck from various Pacific Coast newspapers* (San Francisco, 1869)

............., *California Anthology* (San Francisco, 1880)

Taylor, William. *Seven Years of Street Preaching in San Francisco, California* . . . (New York, 1857)

............., *California Life Illustrated* (New York, 1858)

Upham, Samuel C. *Notes of a Voyage to California, Together with Scenes in El Dorado, 1849-1850* (Philadelphia, 1878)

Watson, Douglas S. *California in the '50's. Fifty Views of cities and mining camps drawn in stone, etc.* (San Francisco, 1936)

White, William F. (Grey, W. pseud.) *A Picture of Pioneer Times in California, Illustrated with Anecdotes and Stories Taken from Real Life* (San Francisco, 1881)

NOTES AND REFERENCES

(1)   Francisco Garcia Diego y Moreno, O.F.M., (1785-1846) first Bishop of the Diocese of Both Californias, (1840-1846).

(2)   Engelhardt, Zephyrin, *Santa Barbara Mission,* (San Francisco, 1923) pp. 217-256:

"On April 25, 1842, the Bishop wrote to Governor Alvarado, and by way of explanation said: 'Although our Holy Father Gregory XVI . . . thought proper to direct me to establish my episcopal seat, build my cathedral, and locate my residence at San Diego . . . ' ". (p. 256) "In the meantime, the Rt. Rev. Garcia Diego, in his narrow apartments at Mission Santa Barbara, was fast approaching the end of his life. The religious indifference of the majority of the Californians, notably of the prominent paisanos, which promised no hope of ever realizing the grand plans with which he had entered the diocese, completely discouraged the Bishop.

(3)   John W. Geary was born in Pennsylvania in 1819. He served during the Mexican War with the Second Pennsylvania Volunteers rising to the rank of Colonel. He came to Oregon on the first voyage, April 1, 1849, bringing with him a commission as Postmaster. He served as Postmaster a short time and hearing that Jacob B. Moore had been appointed to succeed him, he turned the office over to W. P. Bryan who was temporary Postmaster at this time. John W. Geary was the first mayor of San Francisco under the Charter (1850-1851). In 1852 he returned to Pennsylvania, served with distinction in the war of secession, later became Governor of Pennsylvania where he died in 1873.

(4)   Quoted by Gleeson, Rev. William, *History of the Catholic Church in California,* (San Francisco, 1872), Vol. II, p. 199.

(5)   James Allen Hardie (1823-1876) born in New York City. While on the Pacific Coast, 1848, Lieutenant Hardie became a convert to Catholicism. He served in various military posts in Oregon, California, and Lower California. He died in Washington, D.C., as a Major General.

(6)   The original of this letter is in the Archives of the Archdiocese of Baltimore, Maryland, Box 27-A. The present author made use of a precis of this letter kindly supplied him by Sister Gertrude Mary (cf. supra).

(7)   St. Francis of Assisi Church, the patronal church of San Francisco, was founded by Rev. John Baptist Abraham Brouillet on Vallejo Street, between Stockton and Dupont Streets, in June, 1849. Father Brouillet was recalled to Oregon by his Bishop and Father Anthony Langlois succeeded Father Brouillet and was actually the first Pastor of St. Francis Church. (For biographical data on Father Anthony Langlois and John Baptist Brouillet cf. infra footnote 8).

(8)   Since Fathers Langlois and Brouillet were associated together in their important work in San Francisco of establishing St. Francis of Assisi Church biographical details with regard to each are furnished in this same footnote.

Anthony Langlois was born on November 10, 1812, in Saint Pierre de la Riviere du Sud, Montmagny County, Province of Quebec. He was ordained priest in the Basilica-Cathedral, Notre Dame de Quebec on May 1, 1838, by His Grace, Most Reverend Pierre-Flavien Turgeon, D.D., Coadjutor-Bishop of Quebec. He arrived in St. Paul's Mission, Oregon, September 18, 1842, and labored in Oregon until 1848. He then set out for Canada with the intention of entering the Jesuit Order there, but got as far as San Francisco, where, in 1850, he was the popular and efficient pastor of the newly built St. Francis Church, then located on Vallejo Street, between Stockton and Dupont Streets.

Father Langlois satisfied his desires for religious life by entering the Dominican Order at Monterey, California, August 28, 1853; he made his solemn profession as a Dominican at Benicia, California on October 4, 1854, when he took the name of Father Augustine. He returned to Quebec severing his connections with his religious Order and was appointed curate at Grondines parish, 1859-1860, and at St. Hyacinthe, 1860-1867. In this latter year he returned to California. Later the pastor of Half Moon Bay near San Francisco, Father Langlois died at Martinez, California, May 9, 1892.

John Baptist Abraham Brouillet was born near Montreal, Canada, on December 11, 1813. He was ordained a priest at Montreal on August 27, 1837. He went to Oregon as a missionary in 1847 and there served, from 1847 as Vicar General to Augustine Magloire Alexandre Blanchet.

Bishop Blanchet sent Father Brouillet to California in late 1848 or early 1849, after news reached him of the discovery of gold, to beg there for the financial necessities of his diocese. While in San Francisco, Father Brouillet was the leading spirit in the formation of plans for the erection of St. Francis Church. He wished to remain in San Francisco, but Bishop Blanchet ordered his return to the Nesqually diocese. In subsequent years, 1860-1884, Brouillet represented the interests of the Catholic Indians of the Northwest in his capacity as Manager of the Bureau of Catholic Indians at Washington, D. C. He died there on February 4, 1884.

Brouillet did succeed in returning to California for a brief stay, but his bishop needed his services most urgently and hence Brouillet did not have any important influence on the later development of San Francisco Catholicism. But we may not underrate his importance as a founder of the first American parish in the Catholic Church there. The "exeat" had by Langlois refers to the official ecclestiastical permission to leave a diocese. (The above biographical information was taken from a footnote in John Bernard McGloin, S.J., *Eloquent Indian, The Life of James Bouchard, California Jesuit,* (Stanford, 1949)), pp. 12-13.

(9)   Quoted in *Eloquent Indian, The Life of James Bouchard, California Jesuit,* by John B. McGloin, S.J., Ph. D., (Stanford, 1949), pp. 9-10.

(10)   Joseph Sadoc Alemany was born in 1814 in the city of Vich in Catalonia, Spain. At the age of 15, he entered the Dominican Order and was ordained a priest on March 27, 1837, at Viterbo, Papal States by Bishop Pianetti. Because of the unsettled and anti-clerical conditions in Spain at that time, Father Alemany volunteered for the foreign missions. He was sent, in 1841, to the Dominican Province in the United States, where he labored in Tennessee, Kentucky, and Ohio. Consecrated Bishop of Monterey, June 30, 1850, he was elevated to the rank of Archbishop of San Francisco, July 29, 1853. He resigned as Archbishop, December 28, 1884, and returned to Spain where he died at Valencia in 1888.

(11)   Originally the diocese of 'Both Californias' included all of Lower California, all the Pacific Slope from Lower California to the Oregon boundary and was bordered on the east by Kansas, Nebraska, and New Mexico. When Bishop Alemany was consecrated, Mexico refused to permit an American bishop to exercise jurisdiction. Therefore in 1851 Alemany asked to be relieved of Lower California and Rome acceded in December, 1852, but he still retained the vast territory mentioned

above. In 1853 his diocese was divided into the suffragan diocese of Monterey and Los Angeles and the Archdiocese of San Francisco. Everything south of Santa Cruz was given to Thaddeus Amat, C.M., (1811-1878), first Bishop of Monterey and Los Angeles, (1854-1878).

(12)   Joshua A. Norton (1819-1880) was born in England, went to South Africa and came to California in 1847-1848. He became a successful business man and owned valuable real estate. In attempting to corner the rice market he suffered financial bankruptcy as a result of which he suffered a mental disorder. He imagined himself to be Emperor of California and Protector of Mexico.

(13)   For an interesting account of Emperor Norton's life cf. Allen Stanley Lane, *Emperor Norton Monarch of America;* also Albert Dressler, *Emperor Norton;* and Benjamin E. Lloyd, *Lights and Shades in San Francisco,* "Emperor Norton," pp. 130-134.

(14)   Admission of California to the Union, September 9, 1850, ended military government, regularized the state government and gave California representation at Washington.

(15)   Jose Maria de Jesus Gonzalez Rubio (1804-1875), was born in Guadalajara, Mexico. In 1825 he took solemn vows in the Franciscan Order at Zapopan, Guadalajara, Mexico, and in 1833 landed at Monterey, California. From 1838 to 1843 he held the office of President of the Missions and in 1846 became Administrator. The title of "Governor of the Mitre" was a Spanish one; the equivalent in the ecclesiastical usage of today is "Administrator," i.e., ad interim of the See of Both Californias, 1846 to 1850. He was Vicar General under Bishop Alemany being appointed in December, 1850 and held this position until the arrival of Bishop Amat in 1855. He died in 1875.

(16)   Engelhardt, Zephyrin, O.F.M., *Santa Barbara Mission,* (San Francisco, 1923) page 320-323. Hereafter referred to as Engelhardt, *Santa Barbara.*

(17)   Engelhardt, *Santa Barbara,* p. 665.

(18)   Engelhardt, Zephyrin, O.F.M., *Missions and Missionaries of California,* (Santa Barbara, California, 1908-1915, 4 volumes), Vol. IV., pp. 665-666. Hereafter referred to as Engelhardt, *Missions and Missionaries.*

(19)   Engelhardt, *Missions and Missionaries,* p. 666.

(20)   Patrick William Riordan, born August 27, 1841, at Chatham, New Brunswick, received his early training at Notre Dame University, Indiana. He went to Rome as one of the twelve students who formed the first class that opened the North American College, December 7, 1859. He was ordained a priest at Mechlin, Belgium on June 10, 1865. He returned to the United States and served as pastor at Joliet, and Chicago, Illinois. He was pastor of St. James Parish, Chicago, when he received his Bulls from Rome appointing him Coadjutor Archbishop of San Francisco. He was consecrated in Chicago, September 16, 1883, and succeeded as Archbishop of San Francisco, December 28, 1884. He died in San Francisco in 1914.

(21)   *Daily Alta California,* of San Francisco, December 7, 1850, describes Rev. Joseph Vilarassa as "Rt. Rev." whereas this title, which at that time was reserved for bishops, should have been given to Joseph Sadoc Alemany, the new Bishop of California, who is announced merely as "Reverend."

(22)   Engelhardt, *Missions and Missionaries,* Vol. IV. p. 682.

(23)   *New York Freeman's Journal & Catholic Register,* "The Catholic Church in California," (Article in issue of January 25, 1851).

(24)   Pro-Cathedral: As defined in, *The New Catholic Dictionary*, Conde B. Pallen and John J. Wynne, editors, (New York, 1929), p. 791, is, "A Church used as a cathedral in a newly created diocese until a suitable cathedral can be erected, differs in no way from a cathedral as to rights and privileges."

(25)   Juan Francisco Llebaria was born on April 15, 1814, at Falset, Spain. March 8, 1831, he entered Congregation of the Mission (Vincentian Fathers). Because of anticlerical conditions in Spain, he went to France in 1836 and was ordained priest at Paris, December 17, 1836. In 1838 he came to the diocese of New Orleans. In 1850 he arrived in California. On January 21, 1856, he was released from vows as a member of Congregation of the Missions. After 1857 Father Llebaria's career is obscure. It is possible he went to Mexico. (This sketch taken from an unpublished manuscript, "History of St. Francis of Assisi Church," by Peter T. Conmy, p. 55-56).

(26)   Archbishop Alemany in a letter to the editor describing his visit to Mexico published in the *New York Freeman's Journal* & *Catholic Register*, January 22, 1853, writes:
San Francisco, California, Nov. 10, 1852.

"Mr. Editor—I have just a few days ago arrived here from Mexico, which business of importance compelled me to visit on my way from the Council of Baltimore . . . "

Since this letter was written by Archbishop Alemany in San Francisco on November 10, 1852, it may be inferred that the Archbishop returned to the Archdiocese of San Francisco the first week of November.

(27)   "Thaddeus Amat was born in Barcelonia, Spain in 1811. He entered the Congregation of Priests of the Mission founded by St. Vincent de Paul. In 1841 he was appointed music master at Cape Girardeau Missouri. The next year he assumed a Professor's chair in the Theological Seminary of the diocese of St. Louis. For several years he was president of the preparatory seminary at The Barrens. He was appointed to the See of Monterey, July 29, 1853, and consecrated on March 12, 1853. Later the See was transferred to Los Angeles which became his residence. A spinal infection, under which Bishop Amat had long suffered, made assistance necessary and in 1873, his vicar general, the Very Rev. Francis Mora was consecrated his coadjutor. His health failed and he died on the 12th of May, 1878, leaving in his diocese much to attest his zeal and labors:" Shea, John Gilmary, *Hierarchy of the Catholic Church in the United States.* (New York, 1886), pp. 301-302.

(28)   Robinson, Alfred, *Life in California* . . . (New York, 1846), as quoted in Engelhardt, *Santa Barbara*, p. 215, writes:

"Santa Barbara," Robinson continues, "was selected to be the Episcopal See: and plans were drawn up for the erection of his Palace, a Cathedral, a Monastery, and a Theological School. The inhabitants were called upon to unite in forwarding these plans, and the Bishop trusted for the resources to the Fondo Piadoso de California—Pious Fund of California—in Mexico, for their accomplishment. Large piles of stones were heaped up in several places for laying the foundations of the above mentioned edifices; but, as the Mexican Government has seen proper to appropriate this fund to less pious purposes, there they will undoubtedly remain for some years as monuments to the frailty of human speculations."

(29)   John Sullivan (1824-1882) was born in Askeaton, County Limerick, Ireland. He arrived in California overland in December, 1844, with the Townsend-Murphy party. Like so many of his fellow immigrants to California at that time he searched about for a means of earning a

livelihood. He began by supplying fire wood for the galley stoves of the early whalers and for rendering the whale oil in the large iron kettles used for that purpose. In 1846 he was connected with William A. Liedesdorff in supplying whalers and other vessels touching at this port which was a business of considerable importance and quite lucrative. At the same time he was engaged in the business of teaming of which he had the monopoly and was also interested in various other laborious and industrial pursuits.

He seemed to possess an almost prophetic intuition of the future importance of San Francisco and quietly invested all of his earnings as fast as acquired in 50 and 100 vara lots (Vara—Spanish measure approximately 32 inches) which could be bought at that time at from twenty-five to fifty dollars each, and which resulted in his subsequently becoming a millionaire. He was upright and honorable in all of his dealings, pleasant and agreeable to transact business with. He was one of the trustees of the Hibernia Bank of San Francisco. He died in San Francisco July 28, 1882. (cf. Swasey, W. F., *Early Days and Men of California,* Oakland, California, 1891), pp. 159-160.

(30)   *Dublin Review,* Vol. VI, New Series. Pages 26-27.

(31)   Although Bishop Alemany in his pastoral mentions the lot at the northeast corner of California and Dupont Streets "was purchased" all contemporary evidence cites John Sullivan as the "donor" of the property. There is no other evidence to indicate Alemany bought the property.

(32)   *Catholic Telegraph and Advocate* (Cincinnati, July 23, 1853), p. 3.

(33)   Hugh Gallagher (1815-1882) born in County Donegal, Ireland, came to America in 1837. He was ordained in 1840 and assigned to work in Pennsylvania. He attended the First Plenary Council in Baltimore (1852) where he met Bishop Alemany who induced him to come to California. He spent the rest of his life building many churches in the west.

(34)   *The Monitor,* (San Francisco), March 15, 1882.

(35)   *San Francisco Daily Herald,* (San Francisco), July 18, 1853.

(36)   *New York Freeman's Journal,* December 28, 1853.

(37)   *Daily Alta California,* (San Francisco), December 22, 1854.

(38)   St. Mary's Cathedral, in so far as the author can learn, is the first Cathedral dedicated to the Blessed Virgin under the special title of Immaculate Conception as defined on December 8, 1854.

When the Cathedral was transferred (1891) to Van Ness Avenue at O'Farrell Streets, San Francisco, it was dedicated under the title of St. Mary's (Assumption) cf. P. J. Kenedy and Sons, *Official Catholic Directory,* 1949, p. 198.

(39)   *Cathedral Journal,* (San Francisco), November 10, 1890. In a personal interview of a reporter of this journal with Father Harrington, this circumstance was included among the priest's reminiscences of the great day.

(40)   Comella, Antonio Alamany, *Fray Jose Sadock Alamany Conill,* p. 27. This is a Catalan life of Archbishop Alemany, published in Spain; the present author has made use of certain excerpts which have been translated into English and which were kindly furnished him by Sister Gertrude Mary of the College of Holy Names, Oakland, California.

(41)   *Cathedral Journal,* (San Francisco), November 10, 1890.

(42)   *Daily California Chronicle* (San Francisco), December 25, 1854.

(43)   John T. Doyle was born in Ireland, November 26, 1819. He graduated from Georgetown College, D. C., 1838, and in 1853 came to

California and opened his law offices where he was retained by Arch-bishop Alemany of San Francisco regarding properties of the Catholic Missions and succeeded in obtaining from the Governor a ratification of the original title of the Church and the Missions to much of the land they had enjoyed. In 1857 John Doyle was retained by Archbishop Alemany and Bishop Amat of Monterey and Los Angeles to act on be-half of the Church regarding the 'Pious Fund'. Mr. Doyle was a great student, reader and scholar. He died on December 23, 1906, in San Francisco, aged 87 years.

(44)   Charles D. Carter was born in Harlem, New York in 1825. He was in the business of real estate and came to California August 28, 1849 via Cape Horn. He was President of the California Pioneer Society from 1870 to 1871. He died May 26, 1871 in San Francisco.

(45)   Major General William S. Rosecrans (1819-1898) was a celebrated Union General of the Civil War and United States Minister to Mexico, 1868-1869.

(46)   *The Monitor,* (San Francisco), April 18, 1868. (The painting of the Immaculate Conception referred to in this quotation as well as other interior furnishings of St. Mary's Cathedral (1868) were de-stroyed in the fire and earthquake of April, 1906.)

(47)   "Story of a Pioneer of Pioneers—John Sullivan," printed in *The Leader* (San Francisco) December 22, 1906.

(48)   *Daily Evening Bulletin,* (San Francisco), May 12, 1861.

(49)   *Daily Evening Bulletin,* (San Francisco), June 28, 1861.

(50)   The *Daily Evening Bulletin,* (San Francisco), June 28, 1861.

(51)   *Ibid.*

(52)   *Flagging*—This was a term coined by the local press at this time to designate the practice of raising the American Flag over buildings.

(53)   *Daily Evening Bulletin,* (San Francisco), June 28, 1861.

(54)   *Daily Alta California,* (San Francisco), June 29, 1861.

(55)   *Daily Evening Bulletin,* (San Francisco), June 29, 1861.

(56)   *The Daily Evening Bulletin,* (San Francisco), July 3, 1861.

(57)   David Batchelder Cheney was born in Southbridge, Massachusetts, June 8, 1820. He was ordained as a Baptist Minister at Mansfield, Connecticut, October, 1843. He became pastor of the 11th Baptist Church in Philadelphia, November 15, 1852. From Philadelphia he came to San Francisco, July 2, 1859, and preached his first sermon in San Francisco, July 3, 1859. He was pastor of Washington Baptist Church on Washington Street. In 1870 he left California for the East and his records are obscure from this date.

(58)   *The Daily Alta California,* (San Francisco), July 6, 1861.

(59)   Ibid. July 18, 1861.

(60)   Tuthill, Franklin, *The History of California,* (San Francisco, 1866), p. 584.

(61)   Right Reverend John J. Prendergast, V. G., was born in 1834. He was ordained in 1859 and was one of the most distinguished of San Francisco's priests. Monsignor Prendergast is remembered, among other things, for the founding, together with Miss Elizabeth Armer, in 1878, of the Holy Family Sisterhood in San Francisco. He died in 1914.

(62)   *Daily Alta California,* (San Francisco), September 8, 1861.

(63)   *Daily Alta California,* (San Francisco), December 24, 1885.

(64)   *The Monitor,* (San Francisco), October 29, 1890.

(65)   Huggins, Dorothy H., *Continuation of the Annals of San Francisco,* (San Francisco, 1939) p. 72.

(66)   *The Monitor,* (San Francisco), March 30, 1867.

(67)   "This school is for boys, and meets in the basement of St. Mary's Cathedral, and is conducted by the three brothers of the Order of St. Francis, aided by six other teachers and a number of monitors, who received compensation."

      The above quotation was taken from the *San Francisco Directory and Business Guide,* (San Francisco, 1863), Henry G. Langley (editor), p. 18.

(68)   *The Monitor,* (San Francisco), March 20, 1867. On Father Bouchard's life and career, cf. *Eloquent Indian The Life of James Bouchard, California Jesuit* by John Bernard McGloin, S. J., Ph.D., (Stanford University Press, 1949).

(69)   *The Monitor,* (San Francisco), March 27, 1867.

(70)   *The Monitor,* (San Francisco), April 3, 1867.

(71)   *The San Francisco Directory* for· year commencing 1871-1872, compiled and published by Henry G. Langley, (612 Clay Street, San Francisco, 1871), p. 41.

(72)   *The Monitor,* (San Francisco), February 2, 1867.

(73)   *The Monitor,* (San Francisco), February 16, 1867.

(74)   *Ibid.* January 18, 1868.

(75)   *Ibid.* January 1, 1870.

(76)   Woodward's Gardens was a popular resort which existed from 1866 to the late '80s. It was located at Fourteenth and Valencia Streets, San Francisco. A conservatory, zoo, art gallery, and a variety of other attractions served to draw sightseers until a decline in patronage brought about its eventual closing. For a more complete description see *The History of San Francisco,* by Lewis F. Byington and Oscar Lewis, (San Francisco, 1931) Vol. 1, p. 399.

(77)   *The Catholic Telegraph and Advocate,* (Cincinnati, Ohio), December 29, 1855.

(78)   Eugene O'Connell, born in Ireland in 1815, was consecrated there in 1860 as the first and only Vicar-Apostolic of Marysville, California, which vicariate he served from 1860 to 1868. With the formation of the Diocese of Grass Valley, California, Bishop O'Connell was made first Ordinary and served the diocese from 1868 to 1884. Because of infirmities of age, he resigned his See in 1884 and died in Los Angeles, California, in 1891.

(79)   Francis Mora was born in Vich, Catalonia, Spain, November 25, 1827. He was made Coadjutor Bishop of Monterey and Los Angeles, May 20, 1873, and succeeded Bishop Amat on May 12, 1878. He resigned February 1, 1896, and died August 3, 1905.

(80)   Thomas P. J. *Our Centennial Memoir* (San Francisco, 1877), pp. 160-169.

(81)   *The Monitor,* (San Francisco), February 7, 1878.

(82)   *The Monitor,* (San Francisco), February 14, 1878.

(83)   Writing from San Francisco to Father Gonzalez Rubio on October 18, 1853, Bishop Alemany thus communicated the momentous news: "Nothing more is lacking than the ceremonies of the 'Burial of a Bishop,' in order to conclude my career. Actually, yesterday, I received the documents—one, a Bull from the Pope, in which San Francisco is erected into a Metropolitan See; another is another Bull by which I am separated and removed from the See or Diocese of Monterey, and transferred to that of San Francisco; finally, a brief which I am authorized to exercise, before receiving Pallium, what without said Brief I could not have exercised before receiving the Pallium." Bulls dated

July 29, 1853 at Rome and certified with Alemany's seal October 19, 1853. (Engelhardt, *Mission and Missionaries*, p. 710).

(84)　　Bishop Patrick Manogue was born in County Kilkenny, Ireland in 1831, and came to the United States at the age of seventeen. He lived in Connecticut for two years and in 1850 left for Chicago where he spent three years in preparatory studies for the priesthood. The arrival of others of his family from Ireland forced him to seek ways and means of support for himself and them; no future member of the American hierarcy ever devised a more romantic or novel method of reaching his priestly goal. He departed for California and the gold mines, and mined at Moore's Flat, Nevada County. Encouraged by Archbishop Alemany, he went to the Grand Seminaire of St. Sulpice, Paris and was ordained on Christmas Day, 1861. He was the pastor of Virginia City, Nevada, for nearly twenty years, then was consecrated in 1881 as Coadjutor to Bishop O'Connell of the diocese of Grass Valley. Upon O'Connell's retirement in 1884, Bishop Manogue became the second Ordinary of the diocese of Grass Valley. On May 16, 1886, the diocese of Sacramento, with the state Capitol as the See City, was created and Bishop Manogue served from 1886 until his death on February 27, 1895, as the first Bishop of Sacramento.

(85)　　*Daily Alta California,* (San Francisco), January 17, 1881.

(86)　　*The Monitor,* (San Francisco), May 27, 1885.

(87)　　James Cardinal Gibbons was born in Baltimore, Maryland, July 23, 1834. He was consecrated Vicar Apostolic of North Carolina— August 16, 1868. He was transferred from North Carolina to Richmond July 30, 1872 and from Richmond to Baltimore as Coadjutor May 25, 1877. He succeeded as Archbishop of Baltimore, October 3, 1877. Cardinal Gibbons was made a Cardinal Priest on June 30, 1886 and died March 24, 1921.

(88)　　*The Daily Examiner,* (San Francisco), October 24, 1887.

(89)　　Lloyd, Benjamin E., *Lights and Shades in San Francisco,* (San Francisco, 1876), pp. 86-87.

(90)　　Quoted by John Bernard McGloin, S.J., in, *Eloquent Indian, The Life of James Bouchard California Jesuit,* (Stanford, California, 1949) p. 16.

(91)　　*The Monitor,* (San Francisco), September 1, 1881 and September 28, 1881.

(92)　　*The Monitor,* (San Francisco), March 22, 1882. (It is interesting to note that the present Cathedral is now located in the heart of San Francisco's "Automobile Row," Van Ness Avenue, the center of automobile agencies.).

(93)　　*The Monitor,* (San Francisco), March 22, 1882.

(94)　　*Ibid.* December 23, 1885.

(95)　　*The Monitor,* (San Francisco), December 23, 1885.

(96)　　The St. John Baptist Church above mentioned is now in use as the parish hall by Holy Cross Parish, located on Eddy Street between Scott and Divisadero Streets, San Francisco. It bears the interesting distinction of now being the oldest (1854) frame building in the city. A tablet inside the building thus tells the story of the building:

> "St. Patrick's Church in Happy Valley
> Market and Annie Streets in 1854.
> Present Holy Cross Hall."

The history of this old building is unique in Catholic Church annals. It has been christened three times, serving as many different parishes. Originally dedicated as St. Patrick's Church in 1854, it was

90

moved on February 22, 1873, to Eddy Street between Octavia and Laguna. On April 20, 1873, Archbishop Alemany dedicated it as St. John the Baptist Church. Archbishop Riordan used it for pontifical functions from 1885 to 1891. When the new Cathedral on Van Ness was opened, this building was again moved to its present location on Eddy Street between Scott and Divisadero where it served as Holy Cross Parish Church until 1899, when the present church was dedicated. Today it is used as the Parish Hall, and so Holy Cross possesses San Francisco's oldest frame building, still in an excellent state of preservation. It stands today beside the classic parish church of stone and brick, whose towers rise majestically above it, contrasting the present progress and magnificence of the city with the dimly fading past of the days of the pioneers.

(97)   *The Monitor,* (San Francisco), May 5, 1886.

(98)   *Examiner,* (San Francisco), December 10, 1894.

(99)   *Examiner,* (San Francisco), September 8, 1894.

(100)   The founder of the Paulist Community, Father Isaac Thomas Hecker, was born in New York, December 18, 1819, of German Lutheran parents, although his mother became a Methodist. As a boy he was obliged to leave school early and worked from the age of twelve to seventeen years in his brother's bakery shop in Rutgers Street.

Dr. Orestes A. Brownson (1803-1876), at that time a Unitarian minister, gave Father Hecker the first impulse to study deeply into the metaphysical aspect of religion. He read Kant, Hegel, and Fichte as a youth, visited the ideal community at Brook Farm, where he met such men as Thoreau, Emerson and Alcott, and also made a stay at Fruitlands, another such community.

He led the life of an ascetic and joined the Catholic Church in 1844. He was ordained a priest October 23, 1849, by Bishop (afterwards Cardinal) Wiseman. Returning to the United States, he wrote and labored as a Redemptorist. With him were those who afterward were his associates in founding the Paulist Congregation — Fathers Walworth, Hewith, Deshon and Baker, all Americans and converts.

These five men — most of the other Redemptorists being German at that time — agitated the question of establishing a house within that order where English instead of German should be the language in common use.

The house was to be a center of attraction for American novices and a basis for missionary work among the non-Catholic Americans. Without authorization from his American Superiors, Father Hecker went to Rome to appeal his case to the General of the Order. The novelty of Father Hecker's plan was misunderstood and he was expelled from the Order on August 29, 1857. On December 22, 1857, Father Hecker had an interview with Pope Pius IX and with his approval Father Hecker and his five confreres were established as the Missionary Society of St. Paul the Apostle, since known over the United States and Europe as the Paulist Fathers.

(101)   *Paulist Calendar,* Old St. Mary's Church, (San Francisco), February, 1940 Hereafter referred to as *Paulist Calendar.*

(102)   *Ibid,* November, 1897.

(103)   *Ibid,* October, 1897.

(104)   *Examiner,* (San Francisco), December 10, 1894.

(105)   *Paulist Calendar,* January, 1898.

(106)   *Ibid,* February, 1898.

(107)   *Ibid,* June, 1898.

(108)   *Ibid,* February, 1899.

91

(109)   *Ibid*, December, 1897.
(110)   *Ibid*, January, 1910.
(111)   *Ibid*, September, 1925.
(112)   *Ibid*, February, 1940.
(113)   *Ibid*, March, 1929.
(114)   *Ibid*, April, 1908.
(115)   *Ibid*, June, 1909.
(116)   *Ibid*, July, 1941.
(117)   The author is indebted for this information concerning the Catholic Chinese Mission of Old St. Mary's Church to Father Donal F. Forrester, C.S.P. who is preparing a history of the Chinese Mission.
(118)   *Paulist Calendar,* March, 1913.

INDEX

Academy of California Church History, publishers of this book, II

Alemany, Most Rev. Joseph Sadoc, first bishop of Monterey and first archbishop of San Francisco, VII; arrival at Monterey, VII; arrival in San Francisco, 8-9; at Council of Baltimore, 11; at Monterey, 10; consecration as bishop, 8; departure for Spain, 41-43; description of dedication, 19; foresight, 30; journey to California, 8; lack of material comforts, 46; made archbishop, 11; moves to San Francisco, 10; pastoral letter announcing plans to build Cathedral, 13; pious fund controversy, 11; proposes new Cathedral, 47; purchases site for present Cathedral, 47; receives Pallium, 36; refuses to raise flag on Cathedral, 28; Silver Jubilee, 37; misc., VII, 5, 6, 7, 51

Amat, Most Rev. Thaddeus, first bishop of Monterey and Los Angeles, 36

Armstrong, Most Rev. Robert J., bishop of Sacramento, quoted, VI

Bergen, Rev. Peter, C.S.P., 68

Bouchard, Rev. James C., S.J., preaches at St. Mary's Cathedral, 31, 33, 34

Bradley, Rev. Charles, C.S.P., 67

Brady, Rev. Edward Bernard, C.S.P., death 55; first Paulist pastor, Old St. Mary's 55; missions in San Francisco, 54; seeks Old St. Mary's as Paulist parish, 54

Burke, Rev. Thomas, C.S.P., 66

Burns, Rev. Joseph A., C.S.P., 70

Catholic Church in California, ecclesiastical organization before 1850, 7; need of a bishop, 7

Catholic Seaman's Institute, 57

Cheney, Rev. Mr. David B., quoted, 26

Civil War, demonstrations in San Francisco, 24-25

Clemmons, Ella, 67

Collins, Rev. Father Claude J., C.S.P., 70

Craine, William, architect of St. Mary's Cathedral, 24

Culleton, Monsignor James H., makes this book possible, VI

Deshon, Rev. George, C.S.P., 53-54

Diego y Moreno, Most Rev. Francisco Garcia, O.F.M., first bishop of the diocese of Both Californians, plans for building, 12; death, 3

Donovan, Rev. Charles, C.S.P., 69

Dimond, Rev. John J., C.S.P., 66

Dunne, Rev. Peter M., S.J., IX

England, Thomas, architect of St. Mary's Cathedral, 24

Flagging Churches, 25

Forrester, Rev. Donal F., C.S.P., 69

Gallagher, Rev. Hugh P., sought funds for St. Mary's Cathedral, 15, 21-22

Geary, John White, quoted, 3

93

Prendergast, Rev. J., 29, 36
Riordan, Most Rev. Patrick W., second archbishop of San Francisco, VIII; arrives in San Francisco, 48; dedication of reuilt Old St. Mary's, 62; invites Paulist Fathers, 53, 54; proposes present Cathedral, 48; misc., 42, 55
Rubio, Rev. Gonzales, O.F.M., administrator of Both Californias, 7
St. Francis Church, establishment of, 4-5
St. John Baptist Church, temporary residence of archbishop Riordan, 48
St. Mary's Cathedral, bells, 20; burials in, 22; ceases to be a Cathedral, 50; construction of, 18; dedication of, 19; early importance of, 8; how financed, 15; importance of, 51; laying cornerstone (quoted), 15-18; music at dedication, 20; music rendered at, 28-29; school opened, 30; selection of site, 12; social contriution, 35; sordid surroundings, 45, 48; Temperance, Library and Benevolence Association, 32-35; See also Old St. Mary's
St. Mary's of The Assumption (present Cathedral), cornerstone laid, 49; cost of, 49; dedication, 49
San Francisco, "cribs" destroyed in earthquake and fire, 59; destruction of records in earthquake and fire, VIII; flagging churches, 25; University of (graduate school) first printed historical thesis, V; vice, 45-46; vice surrounding Old St. Mary's in 1897, 58-59
Sisters of St. Joseph of Orange, 68
Stark, Rev. Henry I., C.S.P., founder Chinese Mission, 66
Sullivan, Catherine, buried in St. Mary's Cathedral, 22
Sullivan, John, contributions to Catholic Church, 23; donates site for St. Mary's Cathedral, 12
Sullivan, Rev. John J., 52
Towey, Rev. James P., C.S.P., quoted, 62
Vaughan, Cardinal Herbert, quoted, 12; misc., 46
Ward, Rev. Paul, C.S.P., 65
Welsh, Bertha, 67
Welsh, Thomas J., architect of rebuilt Old St. Mary's, 62
Woodward's Gardens, 35
Wyman, Rev. Henry H., missions in San Francisco, 54; second pastor of Old St. Mary's, 55; seeks to eliminate "cribs," 69; misc., 62
Wyman Club, 65